# SET MY PEOPLE FREE

# SET MY PEOPLE FREE

## Inner Healing in the Local Church

*Mary Pytches*

HODDER AND STOUGHTON
LONDON SYDNEY AUCKLAND

*Note:* Biblical references are from the NIV except where indicated.

**British Library Cataloguing in Publication Data**

Pytches, Mary
  Set my people free : inner healing in
  the local church
  1. Spiritual healing
  I. Title
  615.8'52      BT732.5

  ISBN 0 340 40903 7

*Hodder and Stoughton Editorial Office: 47 Bedford Square, London
WC1B 3DP*

# CONTENTS

To my four daughters

Charlotte, Debbie, Becky and Tasha

# FOREWORD
## by Carol Wimber

I first met Mary Pytches in 1981 when John and I visited Chorleywood with a team from our Vineyard Christian Fellowship and witnessed a significant outpouring of God's Spirit there.

We have met many times since, both in the USA and the UK, at their church and ours and at conferences, besides having Mary and David as guests on several occasions in our home. Our friendship has developed through common interests and in particular that of the counselling and inner-healing ministry. We have ministered together at conferences and spent many hours discussing the best way to help people with emotional problems.

It was as a bishop's wife in South America, back in 1970, that Mary first became concerned about the need for inner healing – for missionaries, leaders and church members. She has read widely and thought deeply on this subject and been frustrated by some of the traditional Christian approaches from personal experience. She has had considerable involvement in ministry to others, and she uses examples from these encounters to illustrate her book. For the last five years David and Mary have travelled widely speaking in many churches about the different aspects of the Holy Spirit's work; Mary addressing the subject of inner healing.

In this book Mary gives wise guidance in an easy, straightforward way which should help any church wanting to commence such a ministry. I believe that there will be a growing demand for this kind of help as the Holy Spirit is allowed an ever-increasing access to the lives of those who want to grow in maturity and wholeness.

I am delighted to commend this book.

Carol Wimber
Anaheim, California.

# INTRODUCTION

This book is the result of a layperson's search and experience in attempting to bring some effective healing to many emotionally damaged and hurting people. God's intention is for all of us to be whole. Obviously not everyone can get professional help (which may not in any case be adequate) but it should be possible for some healing to be mediated through the local church. What is written here is intended to encourage those ordinary Christian people who want to be healed and who also long to mediate this healing to others.

Many churches are experiencing a renewing touch from God and are beginning to learn how to minister to people in the power of the Holy Spirit. My husband, David, has already written a basic guide-book to help those wanting to move into a ministry of power in the local church. What is written here is about one area arising out of this larger ministry and as such it would be helpful if his book, *Come Holy Spirit* (Hodder and Stoughton), was read first. For example I have taken for granted a knowledge of the gifts of the Spirit which are spelled out in detail in his book.

Our actual practice of inner healing is developing out of this framework (the ministry of the Holy Spirit). As a church we are continually trying to let God be God and allow Him to direct what we do. In our reading we have also benefited greatly from the insights of others. Though many modern psychotherapies are humanistic in their approach, they have some most helpful insights on the human predicament which are not at variance with the biblical doctrine of man.

In the second chapter I have outlined a simplified way of

looking at people's problems. This view is from the 'Free to Be' course, prepared by Gloria Thompson of the Vineyard Christian Fellowship, California, which we have used here repeatedly to help many people to grow towards maturity.

Personalities are far more complex than the following chapters may suggest and we accept that a professional counsellor may have difficulty with our approach. Nevertheless, given some basic understanding of the human predicament, some underlying values and simple guidelines, more churches could be encouraged to develop a healing ministry to the emotionally damaged. In this way a greater number of hurting people could be helped than would otherwise be possible if it was all left to the professionals.

This is written by a non-professional for non-professionals and I hope I have succeeded in keeping both the language and the approach to this ministry simple. It may appear that I have not differentiated between counselling and inner healing; this is because it seems impossible to separate the two. The ministry of inner healing must include both praying and counselling. Inner-healing prayer alone may not always be sufficient for removing obstacles on the path to maturity. A counselling ministry will go hand in hand with a prayer ministry.

I have quoted from a number of books and acknowledged my sources. In particular I should like to mention my indebtedness to Dr M. Scott Peck M.D. for his book *The Road Less Travelled*. It is the best secular book I have read on growth and maturity. As I read it I kept thinking that this man should be a Christian. I was delighted, therefore, to open his second book *A People of the Lie* to find he had by then become one.

I should never have put pen to paper were it not for the encouragement and help of my husband, David. Alone I would not have taken the risk of trying to encapsulate our present views, values and practices. What I have written is the result of a journey of discovery which I hope the reader will appreciate is still in progress. I owe a debt of gratitude also to Carol Wimber, who allowed me to minister many times with her both in England and America. I am greatly indebted to Patsy Stephenson for typing and re-typing the manuscript and making it seem fun instead of a chore: that's friendship for you! For their love and support I must thank Richard and Prue Bedwell and especially for their help as I have struggled with obstacles from my past that were blocking my own personal growth.

For obvious reasons examples used in the following pages have been disguised in such a way as to make it impossible to recognise the counsellees. The case histories are genuine, but the surroundings and names have been changed. Other counsellees have given me permission to tell it as it was. In any case I thank all those who have trusted me with their inner pain and so have become my teachers.

# 1

# HOW IT BEGAN

At Pentecost five years ago God sent His Holy Spirit upon St Andrew's Church, Chorleywood, in a new way. The experience has caused some radical changes in many individual lives and a gradual change in our corporate life. We are discovering a new delight in worshipping together. Whereas we had always enjoyed Sunday worship we now see it as our ministry to God. The most common New Testament word for worship, *proskuneo*, means 'to come towards to kiss'. We found our worship becoming more tender and gentle as we sought to minister to the heart of God using simple songs to express our love to Him and plain objective language to exalt His name. As we did this our own hearts began to melt towards Him and towards each other. Without having to discard the traditional liturgical structure, worship became 'freed-up' and room was being made for exercising the gifts of the Spirit such as prophecy, tongues, interpretation of tongues, words of knowledge, etc.

After the formal blessing which concludes each service opportunity is given for ministering healing and deliverance in the power of the Holy Spirit. We are seeing some of the same signs and wonders that were seen in the New Testament times. This is a ministry exercised mainly by the laity, and over the last five years growing numbers have become involved in it and by it many have been blessed.

This ministry however is not confined to Sunday worship. It continues all through the week in homes, at places of work and in church cell groups. We have been learning, under the leading of the Holy Spirit, how to minister with increasing effectiveness to many needy people within our parish and to others who come from outside seeking help. As we have given the Holy Spirit opportunity to move in and upon the people by specifically inviting Him to come and do the work He wants to do, sins have been exposed and confessed and many repentant tears have been shed. Also the twisted roots of past hurts have been uncovered. We have had to take time to seek God for answers to this kind of emotional damage. An ongoing informal ministry of inner healing has been developed and some kind of order is being teased out for this.

One of the questions frequently asked is: 'Why is this type of ministry in such demand now when thirty years ago it had hardly been heard of?' Three possible reasons come to mind.

## 1 Our affluent society

The western world has grown increasingly affluent. Even those in the lower income brackets expect to have a number of material goods that were once regarded as luxuries but are now considered necessities. Our basic needs for food, warmth and shelter can be taken care of quickly in the majority of cases, leaving us all with more time on our hands. This has provided the opportunity for asking: 'How am I really feeling inside?' We may dismiss the idea as a useless indulgence in introspection, but the fact is that today our GPs' surgeries are 70 per cent full of patients who just do not feel well. There seems to be no apparent medical reason for this, but these people know they are hurting inside.

During the last year we have seen a number of people referred to us by their doctors who are only too aware that the pain their patients suffer will not be helped by medication. Several GPs have attended our 'Free to Be' courses on personal growth, being as concerned as we are to find some answers to these disturbing problems.

## 2 *The breakdown of family life*

In the past most families tended to live their lives within the communities in which they were born. By residing close together they were available to help each other out with their individual crises. These days families are easily and quickly uprooted and find themselves widely scattered – sometimes across the world. Too many people today, when faced with serious difficulty, have no familiar face to turn to. Marriages are floundering, divorce rates are rising, one-parent families are increasing – some from choice and some through tragedy. Their offspring are suffering. The human problems are compounded. The net result is an explosion in the number of hurting people in our society.

I remember the first cry for help we received on our arrival at the vicarage of St Andrew's. We had hardly moved in before a lady appeared on our doorstep, smartly dressed but clearly distressed. She was shaking, crying and begging for help, though she was not a member of the church or this parish. Her marriage was breaking up, her health was suffering, her child disturbed. Money was not the problem; housing was not the problem; the other woman was not the real problem. She was the sad product of a broken home and had very little contact with her family. Her parents were only too aware of her problems, but they lived far away and didn't want to know. Her long-suffering husband had had enough and wouldn't help any more. She was living in a big luxurious house, driving herself insane and damaging her young daughter, who was also beginning to show similar symptoms. She had tried many physicians and psychiatrists and been prescribed all the usual tranquillisers and sleeping tablets. But they couldn't provide her with the care and support that she needed and would probably continue to need for a long time to come.

Her story could be repeated over and over again. She was a typical victim of our modern society; the sort of person we have all frequently encountered though not necessarily fully recognised.

## 3 The new release of the Holy Spirit's power in our churches

As the power of God comes upon the church our foundations are being shaken. Different forms of worship spring up, new ministries appear and a renewed church emerges. But the church is made up of people and this shaking up by God's power happens to individuals. I heard one Anglican clergyman recently admit publicly that he had cried for three weeks as the power of God touched him. Another friend of ours cried on and off for a year after first being brought into an environment where the Holy Spirit's ministry was encouraged. Hearts of stone are replaced by hearts of flesh.

When we allow the Holy Spirit of power and love to come, He begins to break through our defences for the healing and renewal of our innermost being. The Apostle Paul seems to be thinking along these lines when he prays to God

> that out of His glorious riches He may strengthen you with power through his Spirit in your *inner being*, so that Christ may dwell in your hearts through faith. And I pray that you, being rooted and established in love, may have power, together with all the saints, to grasp how wide and long and high and deep is the love of Christ and to know this love that surpasses knowledge that you may be filled to the measure of all the fulness of God (Eph. 3:16–19).

Whatever the reasons for the demand upon us this has been a

fact we could not ignore. We shall now look more closely at the human predicament and the possible root causes behind the inner pain too many people secretly suffer.

# 2

# THE RATS IN THE LARDER

In 1959 my husband and I went to live, as new missionaries, in a little frontier town called Chol Chol in the south of Chile. We were to share our accommodation with a couple who had already lived there a number of years and the four of us became real friends. On arrival they showed us around what was to be our new home. The kitchen was rather primitive. There was an antiquated wood stove in one corner and a tinny-looking sink in another. With so little to inspect I asked about a closed door leading off the kitchen. 'What's in there?' I asked. Apparently this had been the larder, but rats had got in and the door was kept firmly locked. We lived for the next twelve months with the consequences of this decision: the noises, the smell and the inconvenience. When our missionary friends left on furlough we decided to tackle the problem of the rats. We opened up the larder, scrubbed and disinfected it and blocked up the holes. We then put all our tins and packets of food in there. The larder was in use once more. This story illustrates a common human predicament. Within us we have closed off areas where there lurk hidden problems. We have to choose how we are going to deal with them. We may either keep the doors locked and bolted and live with the consequences, or open them up and tackle the rats within.

These hidden problems can stunt our growth to maturity. They may be identified as mental, social, emotional or spiritual blockages. In the course of counselling many people, we have found these obstacles mostly to be caused by past hurts, irrational beliefs, sin and wrong choices, or maybe all three. We must also remember that the Christian has an enemy who seeks to keep him in bondage. Satan is against our freedom and growth. We should beware of his activity and be prepared for the ensuing conflict as men and women make their courageous bids for freedom.

## 1 Hurtful experiences of the past

These cause fear and distortion and can affect our whole lives. Our past can invade our present and affect our future. Emotions such as anger or fear become attached to past traumatic experiences. An experience today presses some 'hot button' within and we react with the same old feelings – often quite inappropriately. A child who has been sexually assaulted when small may have a distorted view of sex and a fear of close relationships as he or she becomes adult. I have met women who were molested sexually as small children and now flinch every time a man comes within reach – an inappropriate reaction for an adult, but a reflex one that is uncontrollable.

Some people may be able to recollect a particular traumatic event that has caused emotional damage. But for most of us the problem is more generalised and damage is part and parcel of being born into a fallen world with imperfect parents. Isn't this what the Psalmist really meant when he said, 'in sin did my mother conceive me' (Ps. 51:5 AV)? Whether general or specific everyone has some buried inner pain inflicted in early childhood – maybe even from the womb. Deep inside each of us are primal needs for security, self-worth, and significance which have either never been met at all, or only insufficiently. Some babies have lacked adequate food, some have lacked a loving embrace, some have lacked parental bonding. Some have suffered cruelty and some have been left to cry for longer than was bearable.

There are children who have endured the loss of one or even both parents; children who have experienced long stays in hospital, or have been 'evacuated' from parents and familiar home surroundings; some have been deeply wounded by perceived favours to rival siblings. Some children have been sexually violated by a relative, and some molested or sadistically beaten by a parent or schoolmaster. A mother giving evidence against her husband recently in an Appeal Court said her four-year-old daughter would wake up at night groaning, 'Daddy, don't do it!' following incestuous rape by her father. The list of hurts inflicted deliberately or involuntarily by our fallen world is unending. The only recourse for a defenceless child is to repress the pain or terror. The child splits away from the unbearable experience. The pain is left locked within some inner cupboard. Depression, guilt, limiting fear or some type of neurotic behaviour in later life may be the only clue to the hurt within. Once this is detected there is a choice for all of us – either to live with the problems or to walk what may be a difficult and sometimes painful path to healing.

Our *future* may depend on what we decide to do in the *present* with our *past*. The damaged emotions caused by past experience must be healed. We cannot change history, but the feelings surrounding it can be changed by Jesus who is able to transcend time and bring healing to the past. 'Jesus Christ is the same yesterday, and today, and for ever' (Heb. 13:8 AV).

## 2 Wrong or irrational beliefs from the past

These can cause confusion, conflict and frustration in our lives. Starting from a very early age we have beliefs passed on to us quite formally and these can mould the habits of a lifetime. 'Always wash your hands before meals!' 'Don't swim on a full stomach!' 'If you sit on a hot radiator you will get piles!' Many of these beliefs are good and helpful, but others can be damaging and cause conflict in later life. 'Men are not to be trusted,' repeated over and over by an embittered mother, is an irrational and damaging belief for a little girl to grow up with. 'Boys never cry' is a belief often passed on to little boys that can produce unhealthy suppression in later life.

Other beliefs are passed on informally. Watching one's father and mother sorting out problems together is to grow up with a healthy belief that problems can be faced and solved. But sadly we have also stored away many poor and incorrect beliefs.

My parents owned a food business and as a consequence my mother was incredibly fussy about eatables becoming bad or stale. She would throw out food to the birds almost before we had a chance to enjoy a second helping! Watching her do this over the years, I was recording an attitude towards food that would cause problems later in life. When I married and started to prepare meals for others my old belief came out of the store. Living off a missionary salary with a growing family in a Third World country, David nearly went crazy trying to rescue good food before I threw it out!

Yet other beliefs come from past experience. These can be particularly damaging and have a very strong hold upon us. The problem lies with the child of the past who in its immaturity made a faulty interpretation of events. It has been wisely said that 'a child is an excellent recorder but a very poor interpreter'. A child beaten by a bad-tempered or drunken father for just being around, may record the experience correctly but make the faulty interpretation that 'People who are noticed get punished, therefore I must never be noticed'. The fear that accompanied the experience will reinforce the belief and keep it alive, which is why on challenging these irrational beliefs one will often receive the reply, 'Yes, but it's true!' The feelings shout louder than logic!

After experimentation, Wilder Penfield (one-time neurosurgeon at McGill University, Canada) drew the conclusion that the brain records every experience a person has had and also records the feelings which accompanied those experiences. It is those feelings that reinforce the faulty conclusions many of us have drawn about our experiences in life.

'I am of no value' is a belief often uncovered in the course of counselling. It is quite untrue because we all have value and are of great worth to God (Matt. 6:26). When a person 'feels' of no value then as far as he is concerned his experience has simply proved it to be true. Perhaps a mother may have chosen to go out to work to supplement the family income. The child may wrongly interpret that choice as – 'She doesn't care enough to stay with me, I am of no value.' He then continues through life interpreting events in the light of that original belief. The feelings that surface every time anyone is too busy or absent at a moment of need will reinforce that original belief, 'I am of no value'.

Among some of the most damaging beliefs are those we hold concerning ourselves and God. Such beliefs can lock us into childish behaviour which we should have discarded long ago. For example, for many years a person may have used anger as a defence weapon against an abusive father and later against anyone else whom he sensed was attacking him, hurting him, or putting him down. Subsequently this attitude to his father may well affect his attitude to God, giving him a perception which is twisted and untrue. The behaviour pattern of defensive anger will not be broken as long as he sees himself as a victim and God or others as his attackers. His behaviour will start changing when the truth begins to penetrate – that God is in fact his defender who only hurts in order to heal and pulls down to build up – '... the truth will set you free' (John 8:32).

The damaged emotions need healing, but the irrational beliefs also have to be changed. Paul says: '... be transformed by the renewing of your mind' (Rom. 12:2). Unless the thinking is renewed there can be no lasting change. 'For as he [man] thinketh in his heart so he is' (Prov. 23:7 AV). God's word is truth and can free us and renew our lives (Psalm 119).

## 3 Sin and wrong choices

These can plague us with guilt and remorse. We were born into a sinful world. We have not only been sinned against but we ourselves have a bias towards meeting our needs in sinful ways. We have made selfish choices, erected protective structures around us, and chosen sinful behaviour in a vain attempt to make life more bearable. In the process our hearts have become like stone. Our wrong choices are often reactions to what has happened to us in the past. These probably came into effect at the time of the original experience and have continued to develop and change along with our own growth. Therefore in response to a father's abuse a little girl may choose to hate and reject her father and to love her mother. As she becomes adult this may change and become her choice to adopt a lesbian life style (to hate men and to love women). She may also have made the inner vow, 'I will never allow a man to touch me,' simultaneously holding on to an attitude of bitterness and resentment towards men.

The sin and wrong choices have to be faced, understood and repented of. An Old Testament prophet wrote: 'All we like sheep have gone astray, we have turned every one to his own way' (Isa. 53:6 AV). Repentance is a turning away from the behaviour, the attitudes, the choices, with which we have wrongly endeavoured to meet our own needs and a turning to God to meet those needs and be changed by Him.

The focal point of the Christian faith is the Cross where Jesus suffered in our place and died for our sins. It is the place where the repentant sinner finds forgiveness and freedom from his sins. Often a counsellor will be required to bring a counsellee to the Cross of Christ to receive the forgiveness bought for him there. Many Christians know the forgiveness of God with their minds but fail to appropriate it in their hearts and carry a continual weight of guilt upon them. I have frequently encouraged a counsellee to visualise the innocent Jesus on the Cross, to see Him hanging there bearing his sins. When even this has failed to effect release I have sometimes suggested to a counsellee that as he repents and confesses his sins aloud to God he should then take them in his outstretched hands to place them on the Cross suspended on the wall. I have laid my hands over his to keep them there a little time, pronouncing quietly and firmly, 'When you take your hands off you will leave those sins on that Cross of Jesus where they belong, and you are never to take them back again.' Such physical action will often trigger the longed-for sense of release. Nothing is more moving than to see a counsellee, at this point, drop to his knees before the Cross and weep with joy and relief, pouring out his thanks to God.

One of the unique advantages of the Christian counsellor over the secular is that he knows there is an answer to sin and the guilt man carries because of it.

In trying to bring help to those suffering from such hidden problems I am encouraged by some familiar words of Scripture. 'Therefore he [Jesus] is able to save completely those who come to God through him, because he always lives to intercede for them' (Heb. 7:25). Too often the gospel is allowed to have only a superficial penetration and never reaches the inner recesses – the hidden places of our being. I believe that inner healing is helping the gospel to touch every part of the personality. That hidden, hurting child of the past needs to be reached by the warmth of God's love and the truth of His Word, so that he or she may be saved or healed completely.

The following pattern begins to emerge:

ROOT CAUSES   Past Hurt,   Past Experience,   Past Teaching
(formal & informal)

RESULTING PROBLEMS   Emotional Damage
Irrational Beliefs
Sin and Wrong Choices

PRESENT
CONSEQUENCES   Fear, Anger, Conflict, Confusion, Anxiety
Guilt, Remorse, Depression
Neurotic Behaviour
Protective Structures and sometimes Physical
Problems

*Example*
A baby girl is deprived of loving and cuddling by parents.
ROOT CAUSE = Past hurt of deprivation
RESULTING PROBLEMS could be:
Damaged emotions – feelings of insecurity
Irrational belief – 'I must be held in order to feel secure'
Sin and wrong choices – in childhood – attention
seeking, resentment towards parents.
– in present – promiscuous life style
PRESENT CONSEQUENCES – Fear, Confusion, Guilt, Depression

# 3

# VALUES OF THE INNER-HEALING MINISTRY

In his book, *Roots and Shoots*, Roger Hurding traces the secular movement of counselling and psychotherapy back to its roots of pastoral care in the Christian church. God's people have always been commissioned to love one another and to bear each other's burdens. God is restoring this caring ministry to His church again more fully.

In this chapter we look at the values that should undergird this ministry. Values are like the foundations of a building. The deeper and firmer the foundations the better one can build. Without good foundations a house stands in danger of collapse. Foundations in the building industry are like values in the healing ministry – they will dictate the shape, extent and strength of the ministry. The following values are fundamental in our approach.

## 1 We value the work of the Holy Spirit

He dispenses the power and the gifts of wisdom, knowledge and discernment needed for this ministry. We are channels for these gifts. We can heal no one. It has to be God. We always begin by inviting the Holy Spirit to come and we encourage the person asking for help to welcome Him. We may then ask the Holy Spirit to uncover the roots of the presenting problem. We try not to make suggestions however good they seem to us, nor are we too directive with the counsellee, knowing that God's ways are not always our ways and He will uncover those roots how and when He sees fit. Whatever surfaces is what we begin with.

On one occasion a GP brought a sick patient with a problem related to her mother. We invited the Holy Spirit to come. Very soon the patient became aware of problems with her father. We proceeded to minister to this area of relationship. When we had finished and were about to say goodbye the doctor asked, 'When do we deal with the problems relating to her mother?' We could only reply, 'When the Holy Spirit surfaces them.' God knows everything about us. 'My frame was not hidden from you when I was made in the secret place. When I was woven together in the depths of the earth, your eyes saw my unformed body. All the days ordained for me were written in your book before one of them came to be' (Ps. 139:15–16). God knows best how to heal us. Sometimes in ministry He brings into the mind a quite recent memory and deals with that. At other times He may take a person back to a very early experience. With certain deep-breathing techniques it is possible 'to touch off the recall of early "unconsciously remembered" experiences: even the intra-uterine experience' (Frank Lake, *Tight Corners in Pastoral Counselling*). We know nothing about these techniques but as we have invited the Holy Spirit to come He has on many occasions taken people back in time and enabled them to re-experience the birth process (see Chapter Eight). The Holy Spirit can surface memories buried deep in the unconscious. I remember one person asking for prayer having had hypnotherapy. Under hypnosis she had half-recalled a very frightening incident involving a man but had not been able to bring it fully into her conscious mind. We invited the Holy Spirit to surface the memory and in a few minutes the whole incident came clearly into her mind. It was the gardener who had exposed himself indecently to her, and her mother had not responded to her cries of fear.

Our goal is that people will be set free from the chains of the past so that they can be changed into the likeness of Jesus. It is the job of the Holy Spirit to effect this change. 'Now the Lord is the Spirit, and where the Spirit of the Lord is, there is freedom. And we, who with unveiled faces all reflect the Lord's glory are *being transformed* into his likeness with ever increasing glory which comes from the Lord, who is the Spirit' (author's italics) (2 Cor. 3:17–18).

## 2 *We value the authority of the name of Jesus* (Matt. 28:18)

To the man at the gate Beautiful Peter said, 'Silver and gold I do not have, but what I have I give you. In the name of Jesus Christ of Nazareth, walk' (Acts 3:6).

The counsellor must know the authority he has in Jesus. In His Name there is healing for our hurts. In His Name there is authority over the kingdom of darkness. In His name there is power to break bondages that have enslaved people for years. On one occasion a woman told me she found it very difficult to pray for other people or to exercise any ministry in the church owing to a strict religious upbringing in a sect that had not allowed women any ministry. In the Name of Jesus I broke the power that this sect had over her. Today she is ministering very effectively in her church.

## 3 *We value the Word of God*

'Then you will know the truth and the truth will set you free' (John 8:32). The Word of God can minister freedom to those locked into irrational thinking. It can be a light to our path and show up sin and wrong choices that need repentance. It also keeps the counsellor from wandering into error and so safeguards the ministry.

It is important that our practices do not counter Scripture. These may not be spelled out word for word in the Bible, but they should accord with the general tenor of God's Word. It is all too easy to slip into strange practices because they appear to work. I remember someone telling me that she had been present at the vicarious deliverance of an evil spirit. Apparently the person who was supposedly demonised had been present but had not been involved in the expulsion of the demon. Another person present had manifested for him and had then been delivered for him! When I queried this I received the reply, 'But it worked!'

It had certainly been an extraordinary, even exciting, event, but the criteria for evaluating the practice must be placed on firmer foundations than apparent results. At some stage results need to be assessed, but results do not determine our practices. The end never justifies the means. A spiritualist may heal someone but that does not mean we can, as Christians, become involved in spiritualistic healing. Our practices must come out of, and adhere to, our values. The word of God is foundational in this ministry.

## 4 We value love

'Whoever does not love does not know God, because God is love' (1 John 4:8).

'My command is this: Love each other as I have loved you' (John 15:12). Such knowledge and such a commission compel us to get involved in helping others to find freedom and wholeness through Christ. Love must undergird the ministry and govern the manner in which we minister (1 Cor. 13). Each individual is important to God. He numbers the hairs upon our heads and stores our tears in a bottle according to the Bible. The ministry, therefore, must keep in tune with God's heart of love.

For a helpful definition of love I borrow from Dr Scott Peck who defines it as: 'The will to extend oneself for the purpose of nurturing one's own or another's spiritual growth.' Ros, a young mother who is mentioned later in the book, said that one of the keys to her healing from a severe, long-standing, depression was the love of her counsellor who stood by her for so many years and never gave up extending herself in ministry on her behalf. At times this had been costly in time, energy and patience. The turning-point for the counsellee often comes when he recognises that the counsellor really does care for him.

If love means extending oneself for another, the rest of the definition is also important. For what reason do we extend ourselves? Scott Peck says 'for nurturing one's own or another's spiritual growth.' The next value follows on from love.

## 5 *We value the growth of the individual* (Eph. 4:13)

Our goal is not to root around in someone's past out of curiosity or prurience. Our objective is to remove the blockages to growth which may come from the past so that the person is set free to mature.

I remember praying for a married man aged about 30 who was still reliant on his father's help in making the major decisions of his life. His father continually extended himself for the sake of his son. He sacrificed many evenings helping his son run his home and career. The father did not in fact value the growth of his son. Maybe he valued success for his son, or perhaps he needed to be needed by his son, but had he really valued his son's growth he would have allowed him space to grow up and take responsibility for his own life.

In all our counselling relationships and practices we must

be continually asking the question, 'Am I helping or hindering this person's growth to maturity?'

## 6 *We value the body of Christ*

The body is made up of individual parts. If every part works well the whole body will be strong and healthy. 'Instead, speaking the truth in love, we will in all things grow up into him who is the Head, that is, Christ. From him the whole body, joined and held together by every supporting ligament, grows and builds itself up in love, as each part does its work' (Eph. 4:15–16). We value an ever-deepening relationship in the body of Christ. Any ministry should increase openness and commitment not alienate or marginalise a person.

We want to see the Body of Christ strong and functioning powerfully in the world. Jesus said to His disciples, 'You are the salt of the earth... You are the light of the world' (Matt. 5:13, 14). As individuals in the Body are healed, the Body itself will become the salt and light it was intended to be.

## 7 *We value the work of Christ on the Cross*

On the Cross Jesus bore 'our infirmities', 'our sorrows' and 'our transgressions' (Isa. 53:4, 5).
Victory over evil was won on the Cross (Col. 2:15).
Our value to God was clearly declared on the Cross (Rom. 5:8).
Therefore Christ and the Cross must be both central and foundational in this ministry.

With the foundations laid we are ready to start building the house. But before doing so we shall look at those for whom the building is being constructed – those in need of ministry.

# 4

# WHO NEEDS THIS MINISTRY?

However healthy, most people would benefit, at some stage in their lives, through counselling. Birth is traumatic for everyone and living poses many difficulties and problems for us all. Nevertheless, few have access to such help, and many that we see are embarrassed at asking for it, fearing that they are making a fuss and taking up time unnecessarily. We constantly have to put people at ease on this point, assuring them that it is quite normal to have problems and conflicts that are sometimes difficult to resolve on one's own.

The commonest reasons that people have for coming for ministry are:

**(a) Overwhelming feelings.** These include anxiety, depression, fear, anger, confusion, etc. The cause may be a chemical or hormonal imbalance. If this is suspected the person should be referred to the doctor. Often, however, these feelings result from hurtful childhood experiences.

One young man arranged an interview explaining that he suffered from crippling anxiety. During the time together I became aware of a recurring phrase. 'I must never make a mistake.' Eventually I pointed this out to him and asked him if he knew where this irrational belief came from. He thought for a while but could offer no explanation. His relationship with both mother and father seemed good. Realising the cause of the belief was buried in his unconscious, I suggested we pray and ask God to show us where it came from. I prayed and waited. After a short while the man began to cry as if he were again a small boy. Eventually he told me that God had taken him back to his prep school where he was sent at the tender age of 5. In this school rigid discipline had been maintained and the boys were regularly beaten for any small mistake. Fear had taken root in the little boy's heart and whenever he needed to make a decision today the old irrational belief came into play, 'I must never make a mistake,' causing a constant state of anxiety.

**(b) Guilt.** This can be real or false. Real guilt is the result of sin or wrong choices. Only confession, repentence and receiving forgiveness will bring release. False guilt results from irrational beliefs arising out of the past. A person will come, saying, 'I feel so guilty, I must be bad.' After confessing every sin, he still has the feeling of guilt and badness. As he is questioned his irrational beliefs will come to light. 'I was an accident, I should never have been born.' Or, 'My mother wanted a girl – I was the wrong sex.' Or 'I'm a failure; my father spent hundreds of pounds on my education but I could never come up to his expectations.'

**(c) Bondages.** Many people seek ministry because their lives are made miserable by some kind of bondage. These can take many forms.

(i) Habits – people can be in bondage to nail-biting, smoking, eating, masturbating, perfectionism, drugs, alcohol, etc.

When some area of life seems out of control it is always advisable to look for possible demonic activity. But it would be quite wrong to presume this to be the cause without very good evidence. In many cases the underlying cause is one of a very low self-esteem or past deprivation.

(ii) Family – though close family ties are important they can become a bondage if they prevent our freedom to choose or to mature. A grown, married man can be in bondage to a domineering mother. Influences coming down through the family from previous generations can be a problem for some. This could take the form of inherited weaknesses, occult powers, depressive tendencies. On one occasion we prayed for a woman who was extremely depressed without apparent reason. One of those ministering felt there was an inherited suicidal tendency. When she was questioned about this we discovered that for several generations back there had been attempted suicides.

(iii) Religion – this could include a merciless distortion of Christianity, one of the cults or sects. We minister frequently to both men and women who are still responding unconsciously to past erroneous teaching and are not enjoying the freedom and joy that rightly belong to God's family. For example, many would like to exercise the gifts of the Spirit for the benefit of the body of Christ but are not free to do so until the bondage of past teaching has been broken in their lives.

(iv) Words – judgments made on one as a child can keep one in bondage. For example, 'You never get anything right', 'You are no good at maths', 'You are hopeless at sewing'.

One morning a man sat in our sitting-room telling us what a failure he was. Though the story of his life did not bear this out he nevertheless believed it to be so. He was in fact holding down a very responsible position. After much questioning we discovered the judgment he was still living under. As a boy he was an average student and his school reports contained some A's, but mostly B's and a few C's. When his report arrived his father would run his eye down the marks and point to the low ones, berating his son for his failure. There was no praise for his real achievements. The young boy believed the judgment made about him and at the age of 40 was still in bondage to it.

(v) Inner vows – childhood decisions can have a lasting effect on our lives unless renounced and broken. Vows such as 'I will never get married', 'I will never allow a man to touch me', 'I won't trust anyone', 'I won't need other people', 'I will never cry', etc.

Recently a woman asked my husband for prayer because she was unable to conceive a baby, though there was no apparent physical cause for this according to her doctor. During the ministry time she was asked if she had ever made any vow never to have a baby. She was amazed by the question because she had in fact made such a vow early in her life, but had not considered that a childish oath could still be binding on her life. Our experience has been otherwise. Inner vows really do affect us.

**(d) Demonic influences.** The enemy is opposed to our freedom and spiritual growth and will do all in his power to keep us in bondage to the past. Any involvement in the occult needs to be thoroughly repented of and some deliverance ministry could be needed (especially when there has been deliberate rebellion or disobedience to God). We must always, therefore, keep in mind that deliverance from demonic influence may be a necessary part of the ministry for setting the captives free. In our experience most deliverances need to be accompanied by some inner-healing prayer. The counsellors should be very careful not to lay evil spirits on people by the mere suggestion unless there is some very clear evidence of demonic presence. This may be discovered supernaturally through the gift of discerning of spirits (1 Cor. 12:10) or naturally by some combination of the following manifestations: upturned eyes, a strange voice frequently threatening, blaspheming and challenging one's authority, the sudden precipitation of a very bad odour, psychic or occult powers, violent physical manifestation when the presence of the Holy Spirit is invoked. The chapter 'Healing the Oppressed', in *Come, Holy Spirit* by my husband, gives some helpful insights.

Counsellors should beware of requests for ministry from those who want to be 'delivered' as simply a quick solution to their problems, and to avoid the normal responsibilities of living.

**(e) Limiting behaviour patterns.** Fear of small spaces can limit a person's freedom, a need to be continually washing everything is inconvenient and troublesome. Compulsive behaviour of any sort can be worrying even if it is only the need to check on the gas, the lights, or the door locks several times on a winter evening. Many people are plagued by such problems which usually arise from past experience. Though we try not to jump to conclusions in our ministry it would seem that in many cases fear of small spaces goes back to a traumatic birth. We prayed once for a young woman who suffered from claustrophobia. I remember wondering if perhaps she had been shut in a cupboard as a small child and I was almost expecting the Holy Spirit to bring such a memory to light. I was therefore taken by surprise when, during our prayer time, she began to experience a very tight feeling on her body as if she was being squeezed. She became very distressed and for the next half-hour she relived her birth, struggling to come out of that constricted, claustrophobic canal. Writing about 'making sense of syndromes', Frank Lake says that for years he didn't know what to make of the claustrophobic's common fear of being shut in. Not until, using drugs that caused regression, he 'found consistently that the root of this syndrome was the experience of a difficult birth.' (*Tight Corners in Pastoral Counselling*).

(f) **Physical problems** – such as colitis, stomach ulcers, migraines, arthritis, etc. These may often be linked with emotional problems. A counsellee should always be questioned closely about any significant events in his life before the onset of the physical symptoms. Sometimes there has been a very stressful family situation. Often a hurt has been sustained and suppressed instead of being properly dealt with. On one occasion the physical symptom started just after the commencement of an adulterous relationship, which seemed to be more than coincidental and provided a clue to the blockage to healing in that case.

(g) **Power encounter during ministry.** At the regular

ministry times offered during or after church meetings some strong physical manifestations by a person could point to an inner problem. The power of God can come upon a person in the course of ministry and encounter some blockage or stronghold causing a reaction in the body. The stronghold may possibly derive from something demonic, but the surfacing of emotional pain through the Holy Spirit can cause a very similar manifestation in the human body and is, we believe, the more likely cause in our culture. Only experience in this ministry and the inner witness of the Holy Spirit will enable the counsellor to discern.

There was an occasion in our own fellowship when a young girl became dumb and could not speak for several hours. Another person became locked into one position for nearly an hour. Yet another flailed her arms so violently it was dangerous to come too near. These manifestations might have appeared demonic but in reality they were defence reactions to surfacing emotional pain and pointed to the need for some inner healing.

**(h) 'Free to Be' course.** We have run such a course several times in St Andrew's. It lasts for eight weeks (one night each week) and starts by uncovering the obstacles that may be preventing growth and maturity taking place and concludes with teaching on the principles of forgiveness and the practical outworking of this in our lives.

As a result of this course, blockages to growth can be identified (and in most cases quickly dealt with) by the person himself, but for some the obstacles to growth are too difficult to tackle alone and some further counselling is necessary.

This course can be obtained from:

Vineyard Ministries International,
PO Box 1359,
Placentia,
California,
92670.

Our objective in ministry is to bring each person to maturity in Christ (Col. 1:28). The job of the counsellor is to help the counsellee to identify the blockages to growth, to minister appropriately through the power and gifts of the Spirit so that growth, freedom and maturity will ensue. However, the counsellee will need to participate fully if this is to be achieved. He must put his own will to it. The disciplines required for growth to occur should be clearly spelled out to each counsellee before the start of any ministry.

# 5

# THE DISCIPLINES REQUIRED FOR GROWTH

Discipline is essential for solving life's problems. 'Without discipline we can solve nothing. With only some discipline we can solve only some problems. With total discipline we can solve all problems.'

Dr Scott Peck who wrote the above has spelled out the disciplines which he believes are necessary for real growth to occur. Healing is not an easy process. The lazy, the uncommitted and the undisciplined will be unlikely to achieve it. For a successful outcome the counsellee must be willing to try and use these disciplines outlined below.

## 1 Delay of gratification

This is a process whereby gratification or pleasure is delayed in order to confront the pains and problems of life first. The child who hated green vegetables learns that it is best to eat them all quickly and then enjoy the roast meat and potatoes. Gratification is thereby delayed while the less pleasant is first tackled. Gratification is not delayed when the roast meat and potatoes are enjoyed immediately and the green vegetables left to the end. People without such discipline cannot face unpleasantness and pain and will therefore be unable to endure the discomfort of counselling and change. They usually demand quick solutions whenever discomfort is experienced. They are unprepared to delay gratification in order to spend time facing up to the realities that their emotional problems are spelling out to them.

Only on very rare occasions do I agree to see someone on more than a weekly basis. For most the week between counselling sessions is a period of reflection, and allows time for the Holy Spirit to nurture the seeds of healing that have been planted and for the counsellee to take the first steps towards the necessary changes. Occasionally as the Holy Spirit begins to break through the protective layers around the emotions, pain and discomfort may be experienced. I warn the counsellee about this and suggest he keeps busy with ordinary daily activities while praying that the Holy Spirit reveals the root causes of the pain. Usually by the time the next appointment comes round the counsellee has made some good connections with the source of his discomfort and is feeling pleased with his growing awareness and ability to make sense of his feelings.

The delay of gratification however is never easy to put into practice. As soon as inner pain is experienced most counsellees will frequently cry for help more quickly than necessary. Some make the mistake of first calling up their counsellor and if they cannot receive the desired mollification they are then tempted to rush around from friend to friend requesting help. Varied ministry is given which, in most cases, is inadequate and this adds to the confusion of the counsellee. Many counsellors have had the frustrating experience of spending time with such people who have become unable to distinguish between their own feelings and memories and those suggested by well-meaning friends.

On the other hand there are those who will never face up to their problems, but ignore them instead hoping they will go away. Such people are unable to delay the gratification of having peace and quiet now. They would rather put off the possible pain and effort necessary for finding a solution to their problems. Thus, instead of disappearing their problems increase; they become more difficult to unravel the longer they are left. How many couples have put off the discomfort of sitting down together to sort out problems while they were relatively small only to find years later that the ramifications arising from them are almost too big and too difficult to make the necessary changes. They often end up in the divorce courts or eke out an existence under the same roof for the rest of their lives as two lonely and unfulfilled people. It is difficult to counsel those who continually procrastinate; where every painful truth is avoided and any change that requires effort is delayed.

## 2 Acceptance of responsibility

The counsellee must accept that the problems he faces are his personally and no one else's. His problems may have originated from the action or attitudes of other people or some situations or circumstances of the past, but right now they belong to the counsellee and he is responsible for finding a solution. The counsellor is not responsible. The church is not responsible. The minister is not responsible. Counsellees who cannot accept responsibility will be continually blaming others and live in 'If only' and 'Yes, but' land. There is no healing in that.

I well remember a lady in her mid fifties coming for help. She had been suffering from long-term depression and no one had apparently been able to help her. We talked for an hour and during that time she continually laid the blame for her illness on her mother. She recounted a hurtful childhood incident over and over again. 'My mother caused me to be sick,' she said. 'It's her fault I'm like this and no one can help me because I am damaged for ever.' Gently I urged her to accept responsibility for her life and attitudes. She needed to see her responsibility for forgiving her mother. Her repeated reply was, 'Yes, but...' and further detailed description of of the hurt she had received. I eventually gave up the struggle and accepted that from henceforth my name would be included in her long list of those who had failed to help her.

Though it is true to say that a counsellee must take responsibility for his own life it is also true that a person who has suffered emotional deprivation as a child may well be inclined to take responsibility that does not belong to him. He feels that he must have something wrong with him and takes the blame for the lack of love he received. This pattern continues into adult life and he tends to view himself in very depressing terms. For such a person the counselling process must include learning to distinguish between what is his responsibility and what belongs elsewhere.

# 3 Dedication to truth

We can all be incredibly blind to our own behaviour and the impact this can have on others. 'The heart is deceitful above all things and beyond cure' (Jer. 17:9). A middle-aged friend once complained to me that her grown-up children were using her. 'They never seem to grow up and become independent.' She was blind to the fact that her need to be needed had encouraged this dependency in the first place and still did.

Some time ago I had the opportunity to do a temperament analysis test. I felt confident that it would produce a fairly normal result. When it was handed back to me I could hardly believe my own eyes as I read what it told me about a couple of areas in my life. I asked for it to be rechecked. This was done and I was assured that there had been no mistake; when I remained unconvinced I was advised to go home and ask my husband what he thought. I gathered up my courage and put it to him. 'Yes, darling,' he answered straightaway, 'it's quite correct.' Faithful are the wounds of a friend! But acceptance of those unpleasant truths was in fact a turning-point in my life and my first step towards real healing and change.

It is often very difficult for us to face truth, especially when it is painful. In such a case we usually avoid it and unconsciously defend ourselves against it. Without truth there can be no healing and no growth. We do well to brace ourselves and pray bravely with the Psalmist, 'Search me, O God, and know my heart; test me and know my anxious thoughts. See if there is any offensive way in me, and lead me in the way everlasting' (Ps. 139:23–4). A short time ago a young girl said she wanted prayer about a poor relationship with her sister. As she talked I was beginning to feel that the fault lay with the sister. However, during the prayer time when we invited the Holy Spirit to come there was a long silence and then our young friend said quietly, 'It's me, it was my fault.' In coming openly before God she had been shown the truth and she was brave and honest enough to accept it.

## 4 Balancing

To my mind this is the most difficult of the disciplines necessary for growing into maturity. It involves the ability to remain flexible and choose responsibly how to behave in a given situation. At one time it may be right to express your feelings of displeasure spontaneously (say to one's spouse) while on other occasions it is much wiser to wait before expressing them, or maybe not to do so at all. To do something on the spur of the moment may be fun for a Saturday evening, but for a Monday morning quite foolish.

Feelings are good (though they do not all feel good) and are a gift from God, but to live successfully with other people we have to learn to express them appropriately. To be controlled by our feelings is to be controlled by the 'demanding child within'. A counsellee may have perceived rejection by his counsellor. He may then choose to be controlled by his feelings and reject in return. Alternatively, he may acknowledge or confess his feelings to and work with his counsellor to find the causes for them. For healing to occur the 'adult' has to take control.

The 'adult' must take the responsibility for making the right choices. On occasions this will involve the choice to leave behind an outdated attitude, belief, or behaviour pattern. In order to receive some counselling I had to let go of my own long-held belief that I didn't need help from anyone – I could manage perfectly well on my own.

Part of the pain and difficulty of changing involves the 'letting go' of the past. I once ministered to a woman who had been an incest victim. After a while she left me and went elsewhere. Later I met another person who had previously tried to minister to her and whose wise comment about her was, 'One day she will have to give up her identity as an incest victim and take the risk of finding out who she really is.' This 'letting go' of the past in order to 'take up' the new is part of balancing. To these four disciplines we would add one other.

## 5 The commitment to growth and change

This means to search one's heart honestly and ask the questions: 'Do I really want to change?' 'Can I face the risk involved?' Jesus asked the crippled man at Bethesda, 'Do you want to be healed?' (John 5:6 RSV). Sometimes the prison we know feels safer than the freedom we don't know.

Too many people want a short-cut to maturity, but there is none; only sweat and tears! *The Road Less Travelled* is an apt title for Dr Scott Peck's book on growth and maturity. Pain and hard work are not things we opt for easily or quickly. Only a commitment to growth will actually keep us on the road when the going gets tough, but perseverance brings its own rewards as James points out. 'Consider it pure joy, my brothers, whenever you face trials of many kinds, because you know that the testing of your faith develops perseverance. Perseverance must finish its work so that you may be mature and complete, not lacking anything' (Jas. 1:2–4). The effort and discipline necessary to solve life's problems contribute most to our own maturity.

In her book, *Grow to Love*, Jean Grigor says that people in the business of helping folk to change attitudes and behaviour are seeking evidence of the three following factors, which she sees as necessary before any change can take place.

(1) Motivation – a person must want to change.
(2) Permission – a person must allow himself to feel 'this is right for me now – today I can do it.'
(3) Protection – change is always risky especially if it is radical. There is usually some fear of any unknown or unexperienced behaviour or attitudes. It is necessary to look for support or encouragement or some major benefit to accompany the change.

## THE RIGHT TIME

In his book, *Tight Corners in Pastoral Counselling*, Frank Lake interprets the Greek word *kairos* to mean 'the favourable moment, or the right time'. Jesus was always conscious of the right timing for himself. As He prepared to eat the Passover with his disciples he said, 'My appointed time is near' (Matt. 26:18). On another occasion, knowing his time was near but still had not arrived, he said, 'The right time for me has not yet come ... You go to the Feast. I am not *yet* going up to this Feast, because for me the *right time* has not yet come' (John 7:6, 8). A short while later we read of His going up to the Feast. The 'favourable moment' had come. When Jesus heard that Lazarus was sick he knew all would end well, but yet he stayed where he was for two days (John 11:4–6). He was waiting to know the Father's time. Lazarus had been buried for four days when Jesus eventually began to minister to him (John 11:39). We have to be tuned in to God's *kairos* for others as well as for ourselves. We do not want to minister when it is obviously not 'the right time' for it. One way of discerning the proper time is to look for the disciplines required for growth. If these are non-existent or the willingness to learn them is absent, then it is clearly not 'the favourable moment'.

A young Christian woman came to me saying she was feeling depressed and in need of help. Her sad story was a common one of childhood deprivation. In a vain attempt to satisfy her need for love she had deliberately chosen to share her bed with a variety of different men. I asked her if she was prepared to change her life style and allow God to start meeting her needs.

She looked doubtful. I suggested she should go and think about it for a while. I said that once she had decided she was ready to commit to change I would love to pray with her and counsel her. She never came back and later I heard she had changed her bed partner yet again. The ingredients needed for healing were not present. It was not the right time for me to minister to her. I hope it will not be too long before it is.

Once a person has entered into counselling the following advice could help him make the most of the experience.

**(a) Be merciful towards yourself.** At times progress may be slow and you will feel a failure. Accept this as normal. After a counselling session you will feel drained. Take time to rest without feeling guilty about it. Read a book, work in the garden, sew, watch TV or do something creative that will relax you.

**(b) Let healing take root.** When a child plants a seed he is tempted to dig it up the next day to see if it is growing. When the healing love of Jesus is being planted in the heart give it time to take root. Do not keep analysing it or even share it too soon with others. Continue to thank God for what He is doing.

**(c) Take notice of dreams.** Our dreams come from within us. They are messages about ourselves and can often show us the next step in God's healing process. Freud described dreams as 'the royal road to the unconscious'. One young man told us of a recurring dream in which he attempted unsuccessfully to kill another man by hitting him over and over again. We asked God to reveal the meaning of the dream, feeling it held a key to unlock some aspect of the young man's problem. After waiting on God for a while the young man said, 'It's me; I'm trying to kill a part of myself.' We then knew that we had to deal with the problem of lack of self-acceptance.

About three years ago I had a dream which precipitated me into a new and ever-growing self-awareness. I dreamed that I was looking at my own body and to my horror it had turned mauve! My first thought in my dream was 'I was sick!' but then I noticed that it was raining and that the dress I was wearing was soaked. The mauve dye was running and staining my skin. I awoke feeling very anxious and sure the dream was important in some way. Over the next year I dreamed regularly about clothes or dressing and always the dream caused stress and anxiety. Gradually I came to realise that the clothes signified my unreal self that I wore as a public image and that the effort of putting up this front would eventually make me ill. This realisation was an important factor in making some significant changes in my life.

**(d) Be honest with your counsellors.** Fear of being rejected will often keep a person from sharing honestly about present feelings or past experience. Be brave enough to take the risk.

**(e) Echoes from the past.** Sometimes after healing has taken place old feelings may come back and the counsellee is tempted to doubt the validity of the healing. It should be realised that echoes from the past are normal and will occur.

In 1960 we experienced a big earthquake in southern Chile. After the strongest quake was over, the earth shook regularly for many months as it settled back into place. The uncovering of past hurts can be like an emotional earthquake. Feelings take time to settle.

(f) **Remember that change can bring depression.** This is a common experience. Inner healing involves a process of significant change in a person's life. Every accepted belief about life is being challenged. Feelings and behaviour patterns are changing. This can cause a person to be uncertain and vulnerable for a time which in turn may produce depression.

(g) **Take risks.** 'Sometimes you have to feel yourself into a new way of acting, but other times you have to act yourself into a new way of feeling' (E. Stanley Jones). Any healing of the past has to be brought into the present or it is a waste of time. Just as Peter got out of the boat and took his first step on the water, so we have to risk getting out of the past and walking in new ways. If you have always had a fear of intimacy, try sharing a feeling you have recently experienced with the person you know the best. If you have been withdrawn and claustrophobic, causing you to sit in the back row of the church not speaking to anyone, take the risk of moving foward one row each Sunday and speaking to one other person every time.

We may prefer to have a magic wand wafted over us and have all our problems disappear in an instant. Unfortunately this would cause us to remain immature children for ever. The hard work involved in solving our problems matures us and strengthens us. We emerge from the experience with a new self-awareness and self-respect.

While magic wands may not be available, we believe every church should be training people to come alongside those in need with some counselling and inner-healing prayer.

# 6

# THE QUALITIES OF A COUNSELLOR

We receive many calls for help. The need is painfully obvious, but resources for meeting the need seem very limited. Yet in every church there will be some with the potential for becoming counsellors. A good church leader will be on the lookout for such people and seek to encourage their development in this ministry.

What exactly should the leader be looking for in a potential counsellor?

## 1 Natural qualities

Some of these may be there only in embryo and will need developing.

(a) A good listener. He or she must be someone who is interested in people and does not have to talk about himself continually, or need to cap a story with a better one. A counsellor needs to be able to tune in on three levels:

(i) To the speaker. (How does he view the problem?)

(ii) To God. (Is God revealing anything by supernatural means?)

(iii) To any hidden messages. (A person can convey a lot by body language, repeated phrases, irrational beliefs, etc.)

Full attention is needed to accomplish this task. We cannot always produce answers or immediate healing, but we can always listen. If a counsellee has been courageous enough to ask for an appointment, that person should be shown the consideration of a counsellor's full attention. It may be that the counsellor has already prayed with three or four people that day and feels tired. It is helpful to put oneself in the place of the counsellee. He has geared himself up, anxiously preparing to tell his inmost fears perhaps for the first time in his life. To offer such a personal part of oneself to another human being and to be met with only half-attention, eyes wandering to the window, only slightly disguised yawns, or 'I beg your pardon, what did you say?' is to say the least, upsetting.

This came home to me very forcibly one evening in our own sitting-room. I had that afternoon received some rather surprising inner healing. Realising that it was important to share my experience with my husband David and to try and overcome my longstanding dislike of expressing my inner-most feelings, I waited until he had seen the six o'clock news and then said I wanted to tell him something. He turned away from the television and gave me his attention. I started my story. Midway between sentences David suddenly held up his hand and said, 'Hold it just a minute, this sounds important' – not what I was saying, but something he had seen out of the corner of his eye on the TV. In his mind I had all the evening to tell him my story but he had only that one opportunity to catch that snippet of information. Rationally I understood, but emotionally I was devastated. In an instant my experience of the afternoon was devalued and I felt this very personal disovery of mine was unimportant to my closest friend. I'm glad to say David was quick to see his blunder and we talked it through; not only the experience of the afternoon, but the feelings that his apparent rejection had triggered in me. This is all part and parcel of the ever-deepening level of communication and relationship in any good marriage, but as far as counselling was concerned this experience taught me the importance of being an attentive listener.

In her helpful little booklet, *Beginning Pastoral Counselling,* Ruth Fowke suggests the five tools needed by people-helpers are the ability to listen, the ability to listen more carefully, the ability to listen more observantly, the ability to listen more feelingly and the ability to listen more discerningly.

**(b) A loving approach.** It is important to be able to set nervous people at ease. If he is to be trusted with other people's hurts and pains a counsellor needs to be gentle and kind. He will need to have sympathy without over-identifying. Too much touching and holding during ministry can check the work of the Spirit. Love does not mean effusive sympathy. For some sick people sympathy may be more desirable than healing, in which case it is counter-productive.

**(c) A humble spirit.** This will ensure that the counsellor himself is open continually to learning more. The counsellor must be a person who can also receive correction and direction if he is working from a church base. If we are not cultivating humility the temptation will be to blame others for our many failures.

**(d) A precise assertiveness.** This is the ability to state calmly and firmly one's own opinions and directions. To be assertive is not to be aggressive. Nor is it to issue many 'oughts' and 'shoulds' which are counter-productive in this ministry. It means to be able to say 'no' when necessary. This quality will save the counsellor from possible manipulation or control by the counsellee.

**(e) An objective outlook.** This is the ability to stand back and sort through the often emotionally expressed data without being immersed by the feelings of the counsellee or depressed by his possible blame-shifting on to his counsellor.

**(f) A respect for confidentiality.** Every counsellee must be able to trust his counsellor completely. He must know that the smallest secret will never be revealed. Where the counsellor has overriding needs to feel important, the temptation to pass on what is learned about another during ministry will be particularly strong in the local church fellowship. This will need watching very carefully, particularly in a church prayer-group where it would be all too easy, in the course of praying for someone, to disclose their counsellee's hurts.

**(g) A life style of personal hygiene.** Body odour and bad breath can be very off-putting and prevent concentration. The normal attention should be given to this. In such a close ministry it may be helpful to have a supply of peppermints near by. Talking of supplies, a box of tissues should always be available for use by a tearful counsellee.

## 2 Spiritual qualities

**(a)** A personal knowledge and relationship with the 'Wonderful Counsellor' is obviously the top priority. 'We know that we have come to know him if we obey his commands' (1 John 2:3).

**(b)** An increasing knowledge of the Word of God. 'Let the word of Christ dwell in you richly' (Col. 3:16).

**(c)** An understanding of the authority that pertains to a disciple of Christ. Jesus commissioned the disciples and said, 'Receive the Holy Spirit. If you forgive anyone his sins, they are forgiven; if you do not forgive them, they are not forgiven' (John 20:22–3).

This is particularly important if in the course of ministry a declaration of forgiveness or some form of deliverance is called for. At any stage a counsellor may have to break bondages and speak against a lie of the enemy – for all this we need to know our authority. The other side of this is the ability to function easily under one's own church leadership. Our authority depends upon our submission to authority. That is what the centurion noticed about Jesus (Luke 7:6).

**(d)** An empowering of the Holy Spirit and an openness to His continual anointing. 'But you will receive power when the Holy Spirit comes upon you' (Acts 1:8). 'Instead, be filled with the Spirit' (Eph. 5:18).

(e) A facility for hearing God. Jesus was someone who did not jump to all the pressures of either his family (Matt. 12:46–50 and John 2:4) or his friends (John 11:6), but responded first and foremost to his Heavenly Father. Jesus only did what He saw His Father doing (John 5:19). A counsellor must be learning to operate in the gifts of the Spirit, which will enable him to discern what the Father is doing.

If we are honest most of us feel concerned that we don't hear from God as we should. As with most things in life we learn by doing. We need to open ourselves to God and be expectant that He will, at the appropriate moment, place thoughts in our mind that will be of assistance in our ministry. As we offer these thoughts we begin to learn to distinguish between our thoughts and God's. 'The Word of Knowledge' which is of great value in the inner-healing ministry is just a fragment of knowledge revealed by God to help the ministry in some way.

On one occasion a friend of mine was talking with a young girl who had come for prayer when the thought came into her mind that this girl had been sexually molested by her father. Knowing that she could be wrong and that the thought might have come out of her own imagination, she offered it cautiously. 'I think God is telling me that you had a problem with your father.' Immediately the girl began to cry and with sobs she shared her story. 'Not a soul in the world knows about it,' she said. But God knew! And He passed on the knowledge to the counsellor to facilitate healing.

(f) A personal desire for wholeness oneself. To pray for another to be healed when one is still closed to one's own healing is hypocrisy. Jesus said, 'How can you say to your brother, "Let me take the speck out of your eye," when all the time there is a plank in your own eye. You hypocrite, first take the plank out of your own eye, and then you will see clearly to remove the speck from your brother's eye' (Matt. 7:4–5). The context shows that this was addressed to the judgmental. But the same principle applies in counselling. In the process of dealing with our own insecurities and hurts we gain insight and understanding which we may never have read in any book or heard about in any lecture.

A friend of mine suffered the double tragedy of having a still-born baby and then losing a toddler in a drowning accident. Over the years she has worked through the pain and agony of these losses and can testify to the amazing healing power of Jesus. Today she is peaceful with the knowledge that Jesus can reach down into the darkest pit and lift one out into health and wholeness. If I ever have to minister to someone who has experienced the loss of a child, a miscarriage, or a perinatal death, I often call for Jeannie to come and help. Not only does she have empathy with the counsellee's present pain, but she also has the understanding and insight that come from having been through the ordeal of that same pain herself. The counsellee is left with no doubt that Jeannie understands her agony and grief, but at the same time receives the hope that healing is possible because the living proof is there in person before her.

'... we can comfort those in any trouble with the comfort we ourselves have received' (2 Cor. 1:4).

## 3 Intellectual qualities

(a) The counsellor must have accepted the values of the inner-healing ministry as previously outlined in Chapter 3.
(b) The counsellor will need some understanding of the basic counselling skills. This book is designed to help with these, but there are many good books and courses on the subject of counselling. It is helpful to keep up to date in this whole area. The best way to learn, though, is from a personal model. Jesus healed the sick while his disciples watched and

then he sent them out to do the same. An experienced counsellor may invite a beginner to work alongside in a learning capacity.

(c) The counsellor must learn to recognise the extent of his own limitations. A non-professional counsellor needs to know when he is out of his depth. It is no sign of failure to recommend professional help to a person being counselled. (See Chapter 11 on dangers and difficulties.)

A natural desire to help an obviously needy person can sometimes override common sense.

Every summer while living in Chile we attended a church camp situated near a lake or reservoir of some sort. On one particular afternoon I was swimming in a very deep water-hole near the camp where the sides were almost sheer. The non-swimmers were warned to keep very close to the edge. I was swimming quite far out when I became aware of some commotion near the bank. I suddenly realised that a girl there was floundering out of her depth. Wanting to save her from drowning I quickly swam to her rescue though I had no life-saving experience. I came up behind her, still out of my depth, when she grabbed at me out of desperation and I suddenly found myself submerged under her weight. I could not get free and could not breathe. I struggled with all my strength and was within what seemed seconds of drowning when by some miracle my feet touched a ledge and I could raise myself. I was badly shaken, but knew there was no one to blame but myself. There had been other people around I could have summoned to my aid. I should have at least ensured I had a firm footing before I attempted to help her. By trying to go it alone, in such a way, I had put both our lives at serious risk.

One limitation we may face may be that of expertise. Another will be that of availability. It is important not to appear to offer more in the way of time and attention than it will actually be possible to give. To raise a counsellee's hopes only to have them dashed later is counter-productive. It is kinder to be realistic and state clearly, from the beginning, how much support one is able to give. This will prevent unnecessary feelings of rejection and the disappointment of failed expectation in the counsellee.

## 4 Counter-productive characteristics

(a) Some who volunteer for this ministry may not in fact be at all suitable due to an overpowering need to be needed. Instead of 'setting the prisoners free' their ministry will tend to bind the counsellee into a dependent relationship. Counsellors should be alert continually to signs of this in themselves and seek help if necessary before continuing to minister.

(b) Some may be too emotionally unstable. We all have emotional needs and hurts. Some people however are particularly damaged and would be unable to commit themselves to the demanding and often draining work of counselling. The predominance of their own hurts prevents their being objective. As they become progressively healed, however, they may begin to work alongside others and eventually develop an effective ministry themselves.

(c) Some are too judgmental in their attitude. Not only is a counsellor called upon to hear many heart-rending stories of abuse and deprivation, but often the confessions of quite gross sins. Only a counsellor who honestly recognises the depravity of his own heart and understands the potential for sin in his own life will be able to maintain the proper attitude towards such confessions. Looks of shock, revulsion, or condemnation will close up the counsellee very quickly.

(d) Some are too gossipy and cannot keep a confidence. Trust in the counsellor is indispensable for an effective ministry.

(e) One-to-one counselling with the opposite sex is obviously risky and should be strongly discouraged. When inner healing is taking place a person's ego boundaries are lowered and emotional involvement can easily result.

## 5 *The counsellor's responsibility*

**(a)** To provide an environment conducive to healing.

(i) A quiet, private place, away from other people (especially children), the telephone and the doorbell.

Because we live in a vicarage I never counsel there, but use a quiet room in the church buildings. Some homes lend themselves to this sort of ministry more than others. In the past, when I used the vicarage, we contended with the door, the phone and an excitable dog who wanted to join in all that went on!

Some friends of mine have gone to the expense of installing an answering phone to deal with that particular interruption. Perhaps these seem rather mundane and unimportant details. We cannot make healing happen, but we can do a lot of very practical facilitating.

(ii) An attentive and reassuring approach should be cultivated. The counsellee needs to have the full attention of the counsellor and must know that that time has been allotted totally to him.

(iii) A counsellee will feel more secure if the counselling framework is set out clearly. (See Chapter 7: Introducing the ministry to the local church.)

**(b)** To facilitate the healing process by:

(i) Demonstrating open confidence and trust in the work of the Holy Spirit, allowing Him to work and following His lead. We can fail to do this because of a desire to make things happen quickly. Over the years I have been learning the art of waiting, but early in the ministry I was anxious for results. I remember once praying with a young girl called Pat, and asking God to show her the root of her problem. But instead of waiting for Him to answer that prayer I began to interrupt with what I thought were good suggestions 'Go back to the house you lived in . . . Can you see your father?' etc. We wasted precious time as I tried anxiously to help her make a fruitless connection with her childhood. Then I realised what I was doing, repented and started over again. 'Holy Spirit, this is your work. I invite you to come and lead Pat back to any place in her past that you know needs to be healed.' Then I waited, reminding myself that this had to be God's work and not mine! After quite some time, Pat said quietly, 'I can feel the Holy Spirit upon me.' Then she began to tremble. The next moment she was thrashing around in the chair as she began to relive a terrifying childhood experience.

The next time we ministered I was more than ready to wait for God's leading!

(ii) Encouraging the honest admission of feelings. 'How did you feel about that?' is the question we frequently ask. Denial of true feelings will often keep a person in depression and anxiety. It helps to encourage the counsellee either to tell Jesus aloud how he feels about what has happened to him, or visualise the person who has caused the hurt and tell him/her how he feels.

(iii) Allowing the ventilation of strong feelings when necessary.

Frank Lake (speaking of 'Depth Counselling') says:

In Christ, we have been made free and responsible to stay with each other while painful and angry excitations (feelings) are being thoroughly discharged. There is no merit in bottling them up . . . It leads not to health but to internalised tension and the disease of stress. (*Tight Corners in Pastoral Counselling*).

(iv) Becoming directive when necessary. A counsellee should be fully involved in his own healing process and it is the counsellor's job to encourage this involvement. In the case of past hurts, after the feelings have been expressed, forgiveness will need to be released. The counsellor needs to direct the counsellee towards this. Occasionally a counsellee becomes stuck in self-pity and will need to be directed away from this. Confession of sin and renunciation of old attitudes or habits may all need prompting by counsellors.

(v) Maintaining an encouraging and positive approach. We must never lose sight of the hope we have in Christ. The key of promise unlocked the dungeons of John Bunyan's Doubting Castle.

We have dealt with those who need help (Chapters 4 and 5) and with those who will be exercising this ministry (Chapter 6). Now we turn our attention to the guidelines which should make for smooth running, after which we shall look at a possible format for the counselling hour. By offering this we would not want the reader to consider it to be the only approach. To date we have found it the most helpful model for us and one that we feel adheres most comfortably to the values we hold. Nevertheless, we are always gaining fresh insights and learning more as we are led by the Holy Spirit, while we readily accept that the same Holy Spirit may lead others differently.

# 7

# INTRODUCING THE MINISTRY TO THE LOCAL CHURCH

Not only are foundations essential, as we have seen, but so is a good ground-plan. We have laid down the values for the ministry, now we establish a pattern for the local church operable within certain guidelines.

## 1 The traditional pattern of ministry

In most churches where there has been any in-depth counselling it has been in the hands of the ordained staff. In some churches today official counsellors have been especially appointed, though usually not more than one or two.

This has distinct disadvantages:

**(a)** It seriously limits the number of those who can be helped.

**(b)** It limits church growth by using the valuable time of a few which would be better spent on leading the whole flock. In his lectures on church growth, Dr Eddie Gibbs illustrated this point with a graph covering ten years in the life of a particular church. Each year for six years there was marked growth in new membership and financial giving. Then the graph levelled off. He showed this to the church council concerned and asked if anyone had any idea why? 'That was the year the vicar started ministering inner healing,' came the reply. It transpired that this had indeed been the case. Inner healing had become a time-consuming priority in the leader's personal ministry.

## 2 The biblical pattern of ministry

According to the biblical pattern the leader's job is to prepare God's people to serve in order that the whole body may be built up. It is not for the leader to do everything himself, though of course in initiating any new work he may have to play more roles than he would wish. He should endeavour to begin 'equipping the saints' as soon as possible and to facilitate the active involvement of every member in the varied works of service, 'so that the body of Christ may be built up until we all reach unity in the faith and in the knowledge of the Son of God and become mature, attaining to the whole measure of the fulness of Christ' (Eph. 4:12–13).

As the ministry of healing becomes integrated into the life of the local church, several things will start to happen.

(a) The Holy Spirit will begin to break through to deeper areas of individuals' lives. Suppressed hurts from the past will begin to surface and some of those affected will require help.

(b) Some members will be discovered to have natural gifts in the area of counselling and inner healing (see Chapter 6).

(c) Those needing inner healing will be attracted to the fellowship.

(d) The Sunday healing ministry will be the launch-pad for further counselling.

As all this begins the leader will have to make certain provisions:

(i) Teaching on personal growth for the healing and maturing of the whole body of believers should be given. The Vineyard Christian Fellowship (California) have developed good material on personal growth, of which their course 'Free to Be' is one example.

(ii) Those members with special gifting for this ministry should be given opportunity to develop their skills. They should also be encouraged to attend courses on counselling (the Crusade for World Revival runs a very good one). Helpful literature on the subject should be recommended and interaction with others involved in the same ministry encouraged (see book list). This will facilitate a sharing of insights and provide opportunities to learn from each other.

(iii) Guidelines for the outworking of this ministry in the local church will be necessary, such as those outlined below.

## 3 The local church pattern of ministry

Opportunities for inner healing and counselling in the local church may arise in four ways:

(a) **Body ministry.** As the members of the family of God meet with one another socially and in home groups, ministry to one another should become a normal part of their life style. John provided me with a good illustration of this. On two occasions he had received some quite significant ministry in an informal setting. The first took place in a home group at which I was present. We had broken up into small groups to pray for one another and John asked for prayer about his future at work. As we prayed God showed the group, through words of knowledge, that John was suffering from fear that had started back in the womb. One girl in the group had a picture of bombs falling. This prompted John to tell us that his mother had lived in London during the war when she was expecting him. She had in fact been near to falling bombs at that time. As we prayed God assured John that He had been with him even in the womb when his mother had been so frightened by the bombs.

About six months later John and his wife were spending an evening with two friends from the church. Towards the end of the evening they joined together in a goodnight prayer and the Holy Spirit started ministering to John, revealing something more about his fears.

> The Holy Spirit showed me that I had never wanted to be born – I have never valued myself because I was conceived in shame during the war. He also showed me a cast-iron breastplate which I had erected to protect myself against threatening emotions (especially anger) and my father's condemnation towards me in my childhood.

He felt God encourage him to remove that breastplate and trust His right hand for protection. Very gently and in an informal setting God has begun to remove blockages in John's life and put him on the path to maturity. This type of body ministry is the most relaxed and natural form of help for people to receive.

**(b) Authorised ministry in the church.** Many churches today have (like ourselves) ministry times after the Sunday services or other weekday meetings, when people are invited to come forward for prayer. Some who come will be responding to a 'word of knowledge' (1 Cor. 12:8 AV), others will come forward seeking God's help over some spiritual, physical, or emotional problem. The ministry to each should involve two to three people from among the authorised team. They should direct themselves to the presenting problem, asking God to heal in a specific area which could mean one more step towards wholeness for the affected person.

If the person is already being counselled by others, the counsellee or those praying should let the original counsellors know just what has happened. But if no counselling is currently taking place and the person obviously needs further help, those praying should either refer him to a member of the staff, who will arrange for further help, or arrange to see the person themselves, keeping to the guidelines below. During these more formal ministry times we have seen God do truly wonderful things. The first case we spell out illustrates how often physical sickness is linked to some emotional damage.

Incidentally, since praying for the person mentioned below we have ministered to many cases of physical sickness which have been clearly linked to some type of emotional damage. Merely to have prayed for the body could have left a whole area of the person's life untouched. In such cases the likelihood is that the sickness would either never be healed or would return later.

On this occasion we were praying for a lady suffering from a painful rheumatic condition of the hands. I was one of a small team who was praying for her healing. We continued for some time but apparently nothing was happening. After a while one of the team said he felt that the condition was linked to a trauma during her teenage years. When questioned the lady said that she couldn't remember anything particularly bad occurring during that time in her life. However she agreed to our praying that God would heal anything that had been suppressed or forgotten. As soon as we began to do this she started to weep. Her tears fell upon her crippled hands which immediately loosened up and the pain disappeared. God had healed her!

Later this lady wrote to tell me that not only was she physically healed but her whole life had radically changed as a result of that prayer.

The next case demonstrates the variation of this ministry and also the depth to which God can penetrate in a very short time. It happened one evening in our church when the Holy Spirit was moving powerfully on many people. A young divorced woman, named Janet, began to cry and then to shake quite noticeably. Three of us gathered around to pray for her. I had no idea what was happening, nor had Janet, except that the Holy Spirit was obviously beginning something. We blessed what God was doing and prayed for insight. A member of our team of three said she felt God wanted to heal some memories of Janet's marriage and especially those of her wedding night. As soon as this was spoken Janet reacted by shaking more violently and we knew we were on target.

As we prayed that God would release the suppressed pain she began to thrash around and we felt we were all in danger of being hurt. I gave her a church hassock and encouraged her to vent her anger against her husband by striking it. During the next ten minutes she continued releasing years of suppressed pain, anger and disgust against her husband and his mother (who had lived with them and about whom her husband had an Oedipus complex). Janet slowly became calmer and I asked her gently if she felt able to forgive them both. She nodded and with apparent ease released forgiveness to them and received the forgiveness of God herself for those years of stored bitterness and resentment.

This resulted in the peace of God coming upon her and she experienced a great feeling of relief. The longer-term result was that when she again saw her husband she was able to look him straight in the eyes for the first time in three years. She was also amazed to find he was no longer a threat to her.

Now a year after that event her comment to me was that she had been surprised that God had chosen to deal with that particular problem then. It was something she thought she would never be able to face. She was also surprised that it was done so thoroughly in such a short time.

It amazed me, yet again, that the Holy Spirit was able to break through a person's defences so quickly and get to the heart of the problem. Janet had always had difficulty in expressing any anger and her natural reaction was to suppress such feelings. The two key factors, she says, were (i) the powerful presence of the Holy Spirit, and (ii) the presence of three people with whom she felt safe. If body

ministry is the most natural form of help, the more formal
ministry in church must be the most dynamic opportunity
for healing.

(c) **Crisis ministry**. This is done by whoever is available at
the moment of crisis. The crisis counsellor is not involved in
further care unless requested by the counsellee or the
person's regular counsellor. If there has been no previous
counselling and some is obviously needed then the crisis
counsellor should approach the leadership to discuss how
the person may receive more long-term help. The following
story is an illustration of this type of ministry.

One morning I received a phone call from a minister in a
near-by parish asking if I could see Anne, one of his church
members.

Anne had had some recent prayer ministry in her church
following a Sunday evening service. She had felt helped at
the time but since then had experienced problems with
sleeping and had been bothered with some very bad dreams.
That morning she had woken in a very distraught state. I
agreed to see her immediately. She arrived accompanied by a
friend. We talked for a while about the ministry she had
received on that Sunday. Something had seemingly been
healed, but in the process a deeper problem had been
uncovered. Anne had no idea what it could be. I asked her if
she was willing to ask God to show her. Rather nervously she
said, 'Yes'.

I invited the Holy Spirit to come and surface into Anne's
consciousness whatever was bothering her.

We waited. Anne began to shake and cry. This increased
and became quite marked. After a while I asked her what
was happening. She said that she could see a garden. I asked
her how she felt about it. 'I hate it,' she answered, and
became even more agitated. I suggested she ask God to show
her why. At this she began to sob, saying, 'No, no, no, there is
someone there – I'm frightened.' I asked her who that
someone was. 'There are two children,' she replied.

Immediately I felt God tell me that they were Anne's children and they were babies which she had aborted. Gently I asked Anne if she had ever miscarried. She nodded and began to sob all the louder. 'I'm so bad – I shall never be forgiven. They are my babies in the garden.' At this point I had to elicit some more information before ministering further. I asked Anne to tell me about it. At first she couldn't and continued to agonise. Gradually the story of a rebellious young teenager came out. She had twice become pregnant. Both pregnancies had been terminated by abortion. In the telling she again began to cry uncontrollably. I let her express the feelings fully. When she had quietened down I asked her to tell me the names of the aborted babies. (In cases of miscarriage or abortion the mother seems instinctively to know the sex and name of the child.) At first she said she didn't know, but after waiting a bit she named them both. I suggested she talk to Jesus and ask Him to tell the two babies that she was sorry for what she had done. I then encouraged her to confess her sin to Jesus and ask His forgiveness for robbing her babies of life. This she did and I pronounced God's cleansing and pardon in the name of Jesus. I then told her to release the babies into the care of Jesus, which she did audibly.

Finally I asked the Holy Spirit to come and minister the love and peace of God to her heart. Gradually she began to relax in the warmth of God's love.

When she eventually opened her eyes we simply embraced her to signify that she was still loved and accepted in the body of Christ. We ended by talking about the experience and she told me a few more details surrounding the abortions.

During that hour of crisis ministry I felt the Lord had removed a major blockage to Anne's new life as a Christian. In fact she came back later to share what a difference it had made. She may well need some ongoing prayer and counselling, but I felt someone in her own church would be able to cope with that.

**(d) Planned ministry.** This is formal, structured, longer-term counselling and is begun only after certain facts have been ascertained.

(i) If the person is not a member of the local church, the name of his church and minister should be requested. It is clearly preferable for people to receive help within their own churches, but if this is obviously not possible the minister may be approached to find out if he is agreeable to your helping the person. Despite this, his minister could have a hang-up in this area and will neither minister himself nor permit anyone else to do so. In which case the counsellor must use his own judgment.

(ii) If the person is a member of a church home-group it is wise not to commit oneself until the group leader has been consulted. It may well be preferable for someone in the home-group to give the help needed. The group, in any case, should be providing back-up support with prayer and fellowship. There will be opportunity for prayer support at the meetings and someone could be asked to call during the week just to check that all is well. A person going through some inner healing is often particularly vulnerable during the Sunday services. When there is no family support, it could be a loving move for members of the home-group to ensure that he is not left to sit alone.

(iii) If the person has been having counselling from elsewhere, it is important to find out from whom and for how long. There should be no commitment to ongoing counselling if some sort of counselling relationship already exists. Advise the counsellee that one must refer to the previous counsellor(s) before there can be any further counselling. It should never be left to the person needing help to 'make it right' with the original counsellor or home-group leader.

Remember that a person with surfacing needs, who is in some sort of emotional pain, can be unconsciously manipulative, demanding, selfish and often devious. Escape from, or avoidance of, a previous counselling situation may well allow the counsellee to evade facing up to or working through some problem areas which it is necessary to do before he can come into a place of healing.

## 4 Stipulation to the counsellee

It is important from the very beginning to make certain stipulations to the counsellee pertaining to any ongoing counselling ministry.

(a) The counsellee should not be receiving any formal ministry elsewhere while counselling is in progress. This would (i) bring confusion and (ii) cause bad relationships to develop in the local church situation. (iii) It may also mean the counsellee will not face up to the real cause of his inner hurts.

(b) It is desirable that the counsellee should receive loving support from his church home-group and family where possible.

(c) The counsellee should be advised that you will be working with a partner. This diminishes the possibility of dependency, shares out responsibility, provides checks and counterbalances when the gifts are in operation and protects the relationship from anything inordinate developing. Make sure the person has no objections to your choice of partner in counselling, but never to the extent of your being left to minister on your own.

(d) Make your time schedule for counselling clear by the end of the first session, i.e. you will see them weekly or fortnightly. Offer a trial run of four sessions to begin with. The situation should be reviewed later and fresh arrangements made if further ministry seems worthwhile. It could be that another four sessions are required, or that a rest is called for to let the ministry 'settle' and 'take root'. Give the counsellee permission to call back at a later date. If the first four sessions have been difficult and have clearly proved unhelpful, the counsellor should look (i) first to himself and ask God if perhaps he is the right person to help this particular counsellee. A change may be beneficial; (ii) The disciplines required for healing to take place should be reviewed (see Chapter 5) and if it is plain that some of these are being ignored then a termination should be considered – at least for the time being.

## 5 *The disadvantages of the local-based ministry*

(a) **Too ready access of counsellor.** The counsellee may live close by and if some clear guidelines are not spelled out at the beginning he could easily regress and become an un-disciplined demanding 'child'. Therefore:

(i) Ensure the counsellee knows the time of the next appointment so that it is there to look forward to.

(ii) Assure the counsellee that you will be available on the telephone if things become difficult, but this may have to be limited if it becomes more than the counsellor can cope with.

(iii) Talk through the disciplines necessary in order for growth to occur (see Chapter 5).

(iv) Learn to discern when the counsellee needs to exercise some control of feelings and when he may really be emotionally 'on the edge of the abyss'. The information given one during the early appointments will alert one to any possibility of breakdown. A developing under-standing of people will help one discern early on the strengths and weaknesses within the counsellee.

For example, one woman was beginning to recall some terrifying moments in her childhood. The memory of these had been locked away for many years and she had now bravely decided to try and deal with them. Every time she mentioned a certain member of her family she became very distressed and I made a rapid mental note that when these memories surfaced fully she would need someone to be there with her. I realised that this could well happen outside the counselling hour, in which case I should need to go to her as quickly as possible.

Yet another counsellee rang one evening to say that she had just lost control with the friend she lived with. 'I'm going over the edge,' she sobbed. My knowledge of this particular person assured me that she was unlikely to do anything more dramatic than break some dishes. I also knew that to go running in this instance would be to deny her the opportunity of learning what I was trying to teach her about calling out to God and experiencing His help.

**(b) The possibility of breaking confidence.** The counsellee must be able to trust that anything said in the counselling room will be regarded as strictly confidential. Anyone who has a problem in keeping secrets should never put himself in the position of hearing the confidences of others.

**(c) The difficulty of maintaining normal church relationships concurrently with a counselling relationship.** At first this will be difficult for the counsellee. It is the responsibility of the counsellor to make the way easy. The counsellee should be treated in a normal, friendly way, and needs to know that he is always loved. The fact that a counsellee has shared the deepest secrets of his heart should not mean that you have changed in any way towards him. If anything you will respect him more and admire his courage.

**(d) The risk of a dependent relationship.** This may well occur however hard one tries to avoid it. Working in twos diminishes the likelihood. If it seems a possibility:

(i) Search your own heart. Make sure you aren't needing their dependency to feed your own need for significance.

(ii) We seek a therapeutic alliance with an 'adult' not a

parent-child transference. We build up the adult whose task (and not ours) it will be to descend into, identify with, and give recognition and acceptance to their own inner child of the past (Frank Lake).

Hurts in childhood may cause a person to be emotionally stunted. It is as if there is now a small hurting 'child' within. The counsellor's job is not to relate so much to this 'child' within and so encourage dependence, but to build up the 'adult' so that the counsellee can then take responsibility to bring his own inner 'child' to Jesus for healing.

I have had a fairly long counselling relationship with Margaret. She has been through various stages of dependency and was desperately hoping I would be the sort of mother she wished she had had. Recently God has shown her that all her life she has been hoping that someone somewhere would turn up to fill an aching gap – to meet a feeling of worthlessness. She had never felt that she was of any value to the two people in the world who were like God to her – her mother and father. She told me,

> God made me face the fact that no one ever would make me feel okay – even if they wanted to they couldn't reach into my past and make the baby me feel okay. He gave me a picture which seemed to cover all the needs that my parents had never met. In the picture Jesus came to me as a child. He comforted me. He cleaned me. He took off my rags and put on a shining white robe. He helped me tidy my room and then He got down on the floor and played with me.
>
> God left me with the choice of either waiting around for someone else to do all those things for me or of letting go that vain hope finally and for ever, and allowing Him to be everything to me.

(iii) If dependence is not just a possibility but has become an actuality, encourage gradual independence, much as you should your own son or daughter. Those truly in the process of becoming whole will grow through the stages of depending on mummy and/or daddy (see J. & P. Sandford, *The Transformation of the Inner Man*, for a helpful chapter on re-parenting). This is an area which needs careful handling. It can become one of the sticking-points in healing (see Chapter 10).

(iv) Avoid ministering on your own privately to someone of the opposite sex. The ideal partnership for ministering is a married couple. Such couples need to be secure and at one in their own relationship.

# 6 Advantages of a local-based ministry

(a) It fulfils many biblical promises for the Body of Christ.
It is proclaiming freedom for the prisoners (Luke 4:18).
It is binding up the broken-hearted (Isa. 61:1).
It is speaking the truth in love (Eph. 4:15).
It is building up the body in love (Eph. 4:16).
It is walking in the light . . . with one another (1 John 1:7).
It is confessing sins to one another and praying for one another's healing (Ja. 5:16).
It is washing one another's feet (John 13:14).
It is rejoicing with those who rejoice and mourning with those who mourn (Rom. 12:15).

(b) Support is available for both counsellee and counsellor.

(c) As more people open themselves to the Holy Spirit, and to each other, the church as a whole will grow stronger and healthier. Members will grow in love towards one another – warts and all! The light in the eyes shines brighter and faces become open (Matt. 6:22). The Holy Spirit is able to move with more freedom and power in the midst of such open and vulnerable people.

(d) It is under the authority of the leadership of the church. This provides a protection for counsellors and counsellees alike. It provides a check against inappropriate ministry or mishandling. When difficulties arise the leadership is there to be consulted, and should be, especially in the case of demonisation.

Once the pattern of ministry is accepted and the guidelines established we must turn our attention to details of practice.

# 8

# EXPLAINING THE PRACTICE

The practice of inner healing may take place, as we have seen, in a number of different circumstances. Whatever these may be the ministry will usually follow the sequence outlined below, though occasionally the order may change and the time given to each phase may vary.

## 1 Listening time

This will include:
(a) encouraging the counsellee to relax and give clear information about the presenting problem and related history;
(b) observing the body language of the counsellee;
(c) tuning in to anything God might be saying through the gifts of the Spirit;
(d) making a tentative diagnosis.

## 2 Explanation time

(a) Share diagnosis or any insights received;
(b) Describe the next phase of the ministry and the counsellee's part in it.

## 3 Inner search and prayer ministry time

This will include:
(a) specific request for the Holy Spirit to uncover the root cause of the problem and to surface what needs healing;
(b) waiting and watching;
(c) encouraging the counsellee's participation;
(d) prayer according to whatever comes to light during the listening phase and whatever else the Holy Spirit may be revealing.

## 4 Re-entry time

This involves:
(a) bringing the counsellee back to present reality by a gentle touch;
(b) questions such as 'Are you okay?', 'How do you feel?' or 'What do you think God has just done for you?'

## 5 Post-prayer counsel

Suggest:
(a) relevant Bible passages to read;
(b) some appropriate behaviour changes.
(c) give appropriate advice based on the guidelines at the end of Chapter Five.
The ministry will usually follow this sequence but it may change when the Holy Spirit sovereignly begins to work upon a person before there has been any opportunity for the listening or explanation phases of the ministry. In such cases the counsellors need to listen to God, elicit information whenever possible, explain to the counsellee what is happening and the way the ministry is going, at the same time as the Holy Spirit is doing His work of searching out and surfacing any problem.

During one large meeting I attended, the Holy Spirit was

welcomed publicly to come and minister to all present. A young girl near me fell to the ground and began to thrash around, moaning. Those near by immediately entered into phase three of the ministry – praying for her release. To all appearances she was troubled by a demonic presence and those praying tried to deliver her from some afflicting spirit, but nothing appeared to relieve her agony. At this stage I was called over. As I approached the young girl I could see why they felt the problem was demonic.

However the surfacing of emotional pain can produce very similar manifestations to demonisation. I bent over the girl on the floor and took her hand to quieten her down. I then asked her if she had ever been hurt badly by anyone whom she had had difficulty forgiving. She threw her arms around my neck and began to sob out a sad story about a trauma she had experienced some ten years previously. I explained to her that it was the Holy Spirit who was surfacing this problem because He wanted to heal it. I arranged to meet with her privately for further ministry accompanied by another woman. At that subsequent meeting we explained what we were going to do and then we proceeded to pray for her. God came and ministered profoundly to her that day, healing her broken heart. Subsequently we were able to talk about what had happened and suggest ways by which she could adjust her life to match the healing she had received.

On another occasion a lady fell to the ground in very similar circumstances. She began to cry in a heartbroken way. She was unable to vocalise what was troubling her, but her husband explained that she had suffered three miscarriages and had never recovered from the shocks. With this information we were able to explain to the lady how we were going to pray and the part we wanted her to play in the ministry. The subsequent prayer time appeared to bring significant healing to her life. The miscarriages were like three thorns which had pierced her heart. We encouraged her to give the babies names (mothers usually protest at this, saying they miscarried a foetus which had no name, but it is surprising how often we find the mother has unconsciously known the sex and name of the baby). She named them and we released the babies to Jesus. As we prayed, God seemed to draw out the thorns – the chronic pain she had carried in her heart was gone.

However, most of the inner-healing ministry from our church is done by appointment. For those wanting to initiate such a ministry, the following more detailed guidelines may be helpful so long as they are not adopted inflexibly.

At the first session, when the counsellee is unknown to us, we spend time simply getting to know one another. The interview will often cover no more than the first two phases. During subsequent appointments it will be possible to move fairly quickly into phase three, etc. With someone familiar to the counsellors or with someone coming for a one-off appointment it may be possible to move into the inner search and prayer time during the first interview.

## 1 First appointment

(a) Allow one to two hours.

(b) Arrange the meeting to be in a private, quiet place.

(c) A co-worker should be invited to be present.

(d) The counsellee should be given plenty of time to share:
  (i) details of the presenting problem;
  (ii) past history, home background, etc;
  (iii) present behaviour patterns and the choices being made.

(e) The counsellor should be sure he has fully understood. This can be done by reflecting back to the counsellee what the counsellor thinks he has heard said to him.

(f) Listen for recurring phrases, irrational beliefs, past hurts. Observe the body language and what this could be saying.

**(g)** Make a tentative diagnosis.

The counsellor might say something like, 'It would seem from what you have told us that your anxiety is the result of some wrong choices you have made and some irrational beliefs you are holding. These usually come out of past hurtful experiences.'

**(h)** The counsellee should be given the opportunity (with the counsellor's help) to identify the irrational beliefs and to look for the past experience(s) that might be causing them.

**(i)** The disciplines needed for healing to occur should be discussed with the counsellee (see Chapter 5). Attempts should be made to ascertain that the willingness to use these disciplines is present or at least the willingness to learn them.

**(j)** The counsellor should explain what he thinks will be involved in becoming whole.

**(k)** It can then be suggested that the counsellee should go away and think through what has been said. If the counsellee is prepared to commit to change and to grow, he should advise the counsellor and a further appointment can then be arranged.

**(l)** End the session with prayer.

## 2 *Subsequent appointments*

**(a) Listening time**

Opportunity should be given for the counsellee to say what has been happening since the last appointment. He should also be encouraged to share any insights, dreams or feelings that may have begun to surface as a result of ministry.

**(b) Explanation time**

The counsellor may rehearse some of the values he holds (see Chapter 3) and explain how he is going to pray and what he expects from the counsellee during the prayer time. One could say to the counsellee,

'We are going to invite the Holy Spirit to come to you and

surface whatever He wants to heal. Just relax and be open
to God. Welcome the presence of His Holy Spirit and
allow Him to do whatever He wants. We should like you
to share with us any feelings, memories, thoughts, pictures
that come into your mind. We shall tell you if there is
anything we want you to do.'

### (c) Inner search and prayer ministry

'Pray without ceasing' – mostly silently, perhaps in tongues
but occasionally aloud.

*Remember* – our highest value is the work of the Holy Spirit.
He has the ability to bring to light anything from the
darkness and the power to apply the cleansing and healing of
Jesus. Welcome the work and presence of the Holy Spirit
and encourage the counsellee to do the same. Then wait,
watch and pray – allowing God plenty of time.

*Remember* – The counsellee must make his own inner
journey. The counsellors cannot make it for him. They are
there to provide a healing environment and to facilitate that
healing, not to intrude with their own ideas. They will offer
'words of knowledge', or pictures only when they feel sure
they are from God.

The counsellee should be encouraged to describe any
pictures, feelings, or memories which may be surfacing. It
doesn't matter how strange, trivial or stupid they may seem.
If it is only a partial picture, ask God to make it clearer or ask
Him to reveal the meaning. Should the counsellee have
difficulty making a connection with his childhood, and
plenty of time has been given, some gentle prompting may
help, such as – 'Try and visualise the house you lived in when
you were five to ten years old.' Wait for him to do this, then
ask, 'How do you feel about the house?' or 'Where are you in
the house?', 'Is anyone with you?', 'How do you feel about
her/him?' This will only be necessary if the counsellee is
disconnected from his feelings or suppressing them. Once he
has made the decision to open the doors to the past and clean

out the cupboards, he will gradually learn to make his own connections.

*Remember* – feelings connect the *present* with the *past*. On countless occasions I have witnessed people connect up with a past experience through present feelings. We have invited the Holy Spirit to come and waited. Then, on enquiry, the reply might be, 'I feel so lonely', or sad, or anxious, or afraid. As we have encouraged them to allow the feelings to surface, their bodies might begin to curl up as the past memories are gradually released into the present and the baby of the past is crying for Mummy's comfort, shaking with fear of the dark or moaning with loneliness. Later they often comment 'It was so real – it was as if it had been happening to me now.'

Pray that the feelings come fully to the surface. Tell the counsellee gently that it's okay to let the feelings come. If the counsellee begins to cry, do not try to comfort at this point. Encourage vocalising and ventilating (expressing) until all negative feelings about the memory have been emptied out.

The Holy Spirit may be relied upon to show how to minister effectively to what He has brought to the surface.

## Suggestions for the prayer ministry

(a) If the Holy Spirit has brought to light a past hurtful experience and the feelings about this have been fully expressed then it would be appropriate to:

(i) Take the counsellee through the prayer of forgiveness for those who caused the hurt (see end of chapter).

(ii) Encourage him to renounce any inner vows that he may have made as a consequence of the traumatic experience, e.g. 'I will never cry', 'I won't trust a man', 'I never want to get married'.

(iii) Repent of any sinful behaviour pattern that has been adopted as a result of the hurt.

(iv) Break the power of any judgments made over him by a parent or teacher, e.g. 'What a stupid child, he'll never succeed.' We were once praying for a young man of about 20. He had fallen down under the power of the Spirit and was in obvious distress. His legs were shaking quite violently, his teeth were chattering loudly and he kept groaning but was unable to tell us what was happening. Those ministering felt there was some sort of bondage and we prayed generally that God would free him – there was no apparent tranquillising or improvement. Then we prayed that the peace of God would come upon him, but he continued to shake. We all continued praying silently to God for insight when all at once, one of the ministry team said, 'In the name of Jesus I break the power of negative words on your life.' The shaking stopped instantly. He breathed one loud sigh and whispered, 'Thank you, Jesus!' Quite obviously something significant had happened to him. Only time will reveal its beneficial extent.

(v) Invite Jesus to come and heal the memory (see end of chapter). Allow plenty of time at this point. When it is evident that the counsellee is having a real encounter with Jesus leave him to take in the full impact of this. He will 'come back' when it is God's time.

**(b)** If there appears to be a bondage to some person, family or religion this will need to be:

(i) renounced by the counsellee;

(ii) broken by the counsellor in the name of Jesus.

Sometimes the Holy Spirit will indicate a bad influence coming down through the family line in which case:

(i) The counsellee may need to be cut free from his bloodline back to his great-grandparents – three generations.

(ii) Freedom (to be the person God intended) should be pronounced.

**(c)** When the Holy Spirit has brought sin to the light, it is necessary to:

(i) Encourage a full confession aloud to God, in the presence of the counsellor (according to James 5:16).

(ii) Forgiveness should be pronounced by the counsellor in the name of Jesus.

A woman came once and said she couldn't enjoy worship. 'There is always a blockage,' she said. After a few minutes' beating about the bush she finally came out with the fact that she had been involved in a sinful relationship several years previously. Though she knew rationally that God had forgiven her she still felt guilty. 'Could this be the cause of the blockage?' she asked. Some words of Scripture came to my mind. 'Dear friends, if our hearts do not condemn us, we have confidence before God...' (1 John 3:21). I felt that her heart was condemning her and that she had lost confidence with God, so I suggested she confess her sin aloud to God. This she did. I then pronounced forgiveness in the name of Jesus, using the words: 'If we confess our sins, he is faithful and just and will forgive us our sins and purify us from all unrighteousness' (1 John 1–9). I met this same woman a year later and she not only looked different but could hardly contain the new joy she felt in her Christian life; particularly in times of worship.

Where the presenting problem is some sin or wrong choice, the root cause may need to be uncovered. The counsellor should endeavour to discern the need the counsellee is trying to meet by his behaviour. Why is there such a gap in his need for security or self-worth? If the counsellee doesn't know, ask the Holy Spirit to reveal it. Then give Him time to do so.

We frequently encounter evidence of lying, avoidance of truth and exaggeration in our counsellees. It is, of course, always necessary to repent of the sin, to confess it and to receive forgiveness, but to stop there could be to leave the root still untouched. At the bottom of this particular sin is often the experience of conditional love. Parents may have been very performance orientated and dished out acceptance according to performance and perhaps even given punishment for failure. It then follows that failure of any sort brings up feelings of fear. A habit of lying, exaggerating and avoiding uncomfortable truth begins to take root. Until God begins to meet that inner need for acceptance, the habit will be hard to break.

**(d) Re-entry time.** This is important following any time of prayer ministry. The counsellee needs to come back to the present reality and talk openly and about the experience he has just had.

**(e) Post-prayer counsel.** Irrational beliefs arising from the past need to be changed and worked on in the present. Some appropriate passages of Scripture to study may be suggested. Behaviour patterns may need changing. Agree together on some appropriate first steps towards change.

## 3 Further appointments

Another appointment may be arranged if the counsellee feels there is more to be dealt with. Sometimes the ministry may extend over a period of several months or even longer for some. People differ in the length of time they remain in counselling. If progress is being made, however slow, it is worth continuing. We have seen some very profound changes take place with long-term counselling. This has encouraged us to persevere when 'snail's pace' would best describe a counsellee's progress. It is rather like peeling off the layers of an onion and the better defended the person is, the longer it seems to take. For other counsellees, however, one or two sessions may appear to be sufficient. In this case give the counsellee permission to come back at a later date if further difficulties arise.

## *Releasing forgiveness to those who have hurt us*

This is fundamental to the Christian life and to every healing of past hurts.

No traumatic experience in the past is ever dealt with fully unless forgiveness is released to those from whom the hurt was received. This needs to be done even if the hurt was only a perceived or unintentional one. Even if now as an adult it is possible to understand the reasons behind the hurt and rationalise the whole event, forgiveness still needs to be released.

The story of the unmerciful servant illustrates the importance of this. The servant owed his royal master a vast sum of money. When he pleaded for mercy the king cancelled the debt and released him. Straightaway the servant went and found another servant who owed him only a small sum of money and demanded immediate repayment. When the latter pleaded for mercy he was refused and the first servant had him thrown into prison until it was all paid back. When the king heard about this he was angry and he likewise turned the unmerciful servant over to the jailors until he should pay back all he owed.

Jesus ends the story significantly, 'This is how my heavenly Father will treat each of you *unless* you forgive your brother from the heart' (Matt. 18: 21–34).

In the days of Jesus the jailors or tormentors extracted information as to where riches were hidden in order that a debt could be paid off. Today the tormentors that extract payment from us are often depression, guilt, anxiety, tension, fear, etc. These tormentors drive us to dig up the hidden past so that we seek help and they will usually not leave us until we have payed up all our debts by forgiving from the heart.

## *Prayer of forgiveness*

Heavenly Father, I choose as an act of will to forgive... I forgive... for (list offences specifically)... I release... Heavenly Father, I ask you to forgive... for all these things as well and that you do not hold these things against him/her on my account.

I ask you to release him/her.

Heavenly Father, I ask you to forgive me for holding unforgiveness, bitterness, resentment, etc., in my heart towards... I receive your forgiveness now and your cleansing of my heart from all unrighteousness.

Heavenly Father, forgive me for holding resentment towards you for allowing these hurts to happen to me.

Heavenly Father, if I have any more negative feelings stored up within me towards... I ask you to cleanse them from me now. I open myself to replace these negative emotions with the fruit of your Spirit (love, joy, peace, patience, etc.)

Heavenly Father, I ask that you now heal the wounded places in my soul. Heal every memory of those offences so that I can look back on them, realistically accepting that they were hurtful, but also trusting that you, Lord, have healed the hurt. Enable me to use this experience to help others with whom I come into contact.

Now, Heavenly Father, I ask that you bless... with your abundant mercy.

Prosper... in every way, body, soul and spirit.

In the name of Jesus.

It is profitable to continue to ask God to bless and prosper this person until all negative feelings towards him/her are healed. And each time you begin to feel anything towards him/her, use this as an opportunity to bless and intercede for him/her.

## Healing of the Memories

We have stated in our values that God alone can bring healing. 'I am the Lord who heals you' (Exod. 15:26). He works this through the Holy Spirit who can never be boxed in by any formulae or methods. If we will allow Him to work in His way and not impose our own ideas, He will bring the healing with such variety that we shall be continually surprised and awed.

Sometimes the Holy Spirit surfaces the memory of a hurtful experience and simultaneously the counsellee becomes aware that Jesus is present. He then relives the experience with Jesus, giving him the courage to face the hurt, enabling him to release the pain and forgiveness, etc. He knows that Jesus is alongside at every point bringing a full cleansing and healing to the wound.

Others relive the memory, but not until the feelings have been expressed and forgiveness released does Jesus come to heal. It may be just by a word that He speaks to them, but sometimes through a picture or simply a feeling – it could even be through all these three together. The counsellee may see Jesus at the scene of the hurt. Jesus speaks to him and he is flooded with a wonderful sense of peace, joy, relaxation, etc.

Having been in touch with something very hurtful and having done all that was necessary on his part, the counsellee may need to be encouraged to invite Jesus to come and heal. If there is some difficulty at this point the counsellor should make sure that all the bitterness and resentment has been thoroughly dealt with. There may have been someone else that had a part in the hurt and he also will need to be forgiven. Once the poison is all out, encourage the counsellee gently by saying, 'He's here. Ask Him to reveal Himself to you. Look for Him' or 'Ask Him to speak to you.' Be relaxed and don't hurry the counsellee.

Occasionally Jesus will reveal clearly the origins of a

behaviour pattern. He challenges the counsellees to remake the choices and break the inner vows made at the time of the incident.

On one occasion in my own experience a surprising memory surfaced in which I was standing in the sitting-room of my childhood home. I was aged 4 or 5. A little evacuee from London, who was living with us, was sitting on the sofa, clinging to her mother. They were both crying. I stood facing them and found I was despising their weakness, their tears, their interdependence and closeness. I hated to see such a show of emotion. Then I became aware of Jesus standing behind the sofa with his hands outstretched blessing the mother and daughter. I realised I was faced with a dilemma. I had not only chosen to despise them but had continued through life with the irrational belief that the showing of strong emotion was a sign of weakness. Jesus's attitude in the flashback was so warm towards the mother and daughter – so accepting of them. Was I going to continue for the rest of my life despising and rejecting what He accepted, or would I join in blessing what He was blessing? For a time I struggled with the choice. Then I repented of my attitude. I renounced the inner vow never to show such weakness myself. I then moved to take up my position beside Jesus, laying my hands with His hands upon the heads of the mother and child. It was for me an incredibly releasing and healing moment.

It has been, many times, my privilege to be with people when they experience such healing encounters with Jesus. I am delighted at the joy and peace these bring, but they are only a beginning of the healing process and too much emphasis should not be put on the subjective experience. Time needs to be taken so that the healing may be brought into the counsellee's present. We must ask, 'What is the truth behind the experience that I must now learn to live in?' The truth for me was that God desires a heart of flesh in place of a heart of stone (Ezek. 36:26). A heart that can not only feel its own wounds but can feel the wounds of others and be able to weep with those that weep (Rom. 12:14–15). I have to make this a new reality in my life otherwise the effects of the healing encounter may gradually evaporate.

People with a strong commitment to becoming whole will usually take these steps towards change with determination and some enthusiasm. Recently a young woman we were helping went through a very moving experience of healing. The Holy Spirit took her back to her birth and then the post-natal experience of being laid in a cot alone. In great discomfort she writhed about feeling unhappy and dissatisfied. Nothing seemed to comfort her. We asked Jesus to come to the little baby. After a while the woman whispered, 'He's come and He has brought a present in a box for me.' We were curious to know what was in the box, but she did not immediately enlighten us. The present was so beautiful apparently that our friend began to weep and for several minutes could not speak about what she was seeing. Finally she told us that the box had contained a crown, which was being unwrapped for her, with shimmering jewels fit for a princess – the daughter of a king!

A month later I met her again looking very attractive. She told me that she had decided that if she was the daughter of a king she ought to look like one! She had spent an enjoyable day out with a more fashion-conscious friend being fitted out with a bright up-to-date wardrobe. What could have remained a beautiful memory had become a living reality because of her commitment to change.

## The birth experience

Not every counsellee has to relive his birth and we have not encouraged him to do so unless God has prompted us in some way. But it may be that the counsellee begins to share feelings of being squeezed or seeing a dark tunnel, etc. Then as the feelings are allowed to surface fully he may roll on to the floor and without any suggestion from us relive his birth. Sometimes the counsellee begins to share feelings of being very small or of being just a blob. If this happens we would pray the person through the time in the womb from conception to birth, taking plenty of time and stopping to allow any feelings to be fully expressed. It is important to emphasise continually the presence of Jesus with them in this; also to recognise that many of the feelings may be coming through from the mother and not belong to the baby at all. So an important stage will be cutting the baby free from the mother emotionally as the cutting of the umbilical cord is relived.

A counsellee may not always regress sufficiently for a direct reliving of the womb and birth experience. Even if this is not possible, an imaginary journey can bring a degree of healing in this area. However, full regression enables the counsellee to connect with hitherto incomprehensible feelings in their original context and with this experience comes understanding, acceptance and reconciliation. One counsellee had all her life felt animosity towards her mother and had not been able to understand why. As she relived her birth, feelings of anger towards her mother surfaced. 'It's her fault I'm suffering,' she cried. With this surprising revelation the root of her animosity became clear. Acceptance and later reconciliation with her mother were then possible.

While being alongside someone going through such an incredible rebirthing I have been so grateful for the truths we find in Psalms 22 and 139. 'Yet you brought me out of the womb; you made me trust in you even at my mother's breast. From birth I was cast upon you; from my mother's womb you have been my God' (22:9–10). 'For you created my inmost being; you knit me together in my mother's womb.' (139:13).

# 9

# TRUE MATURITY

As already explained, the purpose of this ministry is to identify the obstacles to personal growth, to minister appropriately so that healing and freedom will ensue and each person be brought further along the road to maturity in Christ (Col. 1:28).

## 1 Inadequate goals

People seek counselling with very differing goals in mind. Some come looking for relief from emotional pain, some wanting to be rid of anxiety symptoms, others are desperate for help to climb out of the pit of depression. Few come wanting to change their un-Christlike behaviour or remove obstacles to growth or maturity. Nevertheless, the counsellor needs to keep this clearly to the fore in his own mind. A counsellee may begin with the aim of gaining relief, attaining happiness, or being healed of something, but for the ministry to have any lasting benefit he will need, at some stage, to set his sights on the higher goal of maturity.

## 2 Misconceptions of Maturity

What in fact is meant by maturity and wholeness? The following are some mistaken ideas:

**(a) Freedom from pain**. We shall never, in this life, be completely free of pain. Pain and suffering are an integral part of living. 'Life is a series of problems – life is always difficult and is full of pain as well as joy' (Dr Scott Peck). Neurosis is a way of escape from the pain of living, so freedom from neurosis will come with the ability to confront life with all its pain and problems.

**(b) Being better defended.** Being well defended usually means that our 'bad' feelings, such as anger, fear, sadness, anxiety, etc. have been suppressed. Though this may give a good outward appearance, the inside story is bad news! Suppressed emotions usually show up in disguised forms, such as headaches, ulcers, bowel problems, etc. At boarding-school my outward image was that of a self-sufficient leader, well in control of my emotions. The nightly treks along the dark corridors with 'nervous tummy' would have told another story to anyone who was awake enough to notice.

**(c) Acquisition of information.** The western world is very education orientated. We put a high value on being well informed. The acquisition of university degrees is highly prized. Yet a degree will not necessarily make one a better mother, father, husband, wife, son, daughter, neighbour or Christian. Nothing illustrates this better than the case of Dibs. His story – a kind of popular classic – has been written for us by his successful psychotherapist, Virginia Axline. Dibs was a five-year-old who would neither communicate nor play and was considered by his parents to be mentally defective, but therapy revealed that the boy had been acutely rejected, deprived and imprisoned by his own fear and rage. He was, in fact, a brilliant child like his parents. His mother was achieving distinction as a heart surgeon and had perfected two very complicated operations. His father was already nationally renowned for his brilliance. 'All our values,' the mother said, 'had been steadily slanted in the direction of fine, precise, noteworthy intellectual achievement.' Though so well developed intellectually they were both emotionally, sadly retarded parents. 'If I . . . fathom all mysteries and all knowledge . . . but have not love, I gain nothing' (Cor. 13:2).

**(d) Super-spirituality.** Being so heavenly minded that we are no earthly use is not maturity. It is possible to adopt a spirituality that is in fact an escape from real-life issues. A friend once confided that she was on the verge of a breakdown. She had a missionary family staying with her. Every morning the couple disappeared to their bedroom upstairs to have a prolonged prayer time leaving their 2-year-old child to wreak havoc on both the house and my friend's nerves! 'What can I say? They are so spiritual' was my friend's comment. 'But they are not very thoughtful or mature,' was my response.

Jesus was a very human person. He wept, He was thirsty, He was tired, He was angry, He suffered, He loved. He never made a big show of fasting or praying, yet He always said and did what His Father wanted. By His incarnation He showed us how to be naturally supernatural.

## 3 True maturity

We may begin to see an answer as to what is maturity and wholeness in the words of St Paul. 'When I was a child, I talked like a child, I thought like a child, I reasoned like a child. When I became a man [mature], I put childish ways behind me' (1 Cor. 13:11).

A person is mature when he is fully developed, grown up in every way, having left his childish ways behind him. A person is whole when every part of him is integrated and functioning as God intended.

These parts are:

**(a) Physical.** Most of us have attained physical maturity by about the age of 18 without much effort, but it takes understanding and discipline to maintain good health.

Physical health affects other parts of our being. When I had hepatitis once in Chile I became depressed and even lost my desire to pray. The liver infection affected both the emotional and spiritual sides of my life.

**(b) Social**. We were born to relate to one another. Social maturity involves just that – being at home with other people, their company and their opinions. It is also being able to give and receive from others. It is being honest with oneself and others about oneself. It is being able to receive truth from others about oneself. 'But if we walk in the light, as he is in the light, we have fellowship with one another . . .' (1 John 1:7).

It also means being sincere – literally 'without wax'. Sometimes vendors would sell their marble with its flaws filled in with wax and thus deceive the purchaser. Marble without wax was genuine through and through. It was honestly what it appeared to be . . . sincere.

The socially mature person can be assertive without being aggressive. He does not have to be always pleasing others, living up to expectations imposed on him, or responding to emotional pressures from others. He is able to accept other people even whilst he may honestly differ from them.

**(c) Mental**. Mental maturity is being open to new ideas; new ways of doing things. It is being flexible and willing to change. 'Mental maturity involves the ability to take in facts and then reason with them so as to make a mature response' ('Free to Be'). A mature person can take risks and does not evade responsibility for his own life.

**(d) Emotional**. To be emotionally whole is to be a fully feeling person. Many people are very damaged in this area of their lives and are either living with suppressed feelings or dominated by uncontrollable feelings.

'I will give you a new heart and put a new spirit in you; I will remove from you your heart of stone and give you a heart of flesh' (Ezek. 36:26).

Emotional maturity is neither suppressing nor overly

expressing feelings. It is accepting feelings as a gift of God. It is being able to face up to, identify and acknowledge feelings, both hard and good ones and then being able to express them appropriately.

The stiff upper lip has been greatly admired in our culture and in consequence the English suffer from a great deal of suppression. It takes courage to be real and vulnerable. At a recent conference the speaker was describing an experience he had had at a small church gathering. A topic of conversation came up which he knew could touch on a very painful area for him. As leader he had the choice of either changing the subject or letting the discussion continue and risking the chance of breaking down. He made the courageous decision not to change the subject, and to be vulnerable, thus manifesting a 'heart of flesh'.

**(e) Spiritual.** Spiritual maturity means the ability to love God, maintain an open relationship with Him and obey Him. Its spin-off is freedom to accept oneself as chosen and beloved by God, to accept one's gifts and be able to use them for the benefit of others. Quite simply, spiritual maturity is becoming more like Jesus, who was perfectly in tune with His heavenly Father, with Himself and with His friends.

## 4 Free will

In the preface to *Man's Search for Meaning* by Viktor Frankl (a Jewish victim of Nazi incarceration), Gordon Allport reflects profoundly: 'In the concentration camp every circumstance conspires to make the prisoner lose his hold. All the familiar goals in life are snatched away. What alone remains is "The last of human freedoms" – the ability to "choose one's attitude in a given set of circumstances."'

The beginning of our present human predicament was Adam's misuse of that God-given freedom to choose. God has never withdrawn this freedom. Maturity is choosing

God's way instead of our own. 'Deny yourself and follow me,' said Jesus (Matt. 16:24). Putting away childish ways is choosing to leave behind our accustomed attitudes and behaviour and replacing them with something more Christlike. The inner-healing ministry should facilitate the exercise of right choices by unravelling the causes behind the old behaviour patterns. When healing and truth have been applied to these root causes, new choices for good, affecting the present and the future, should be possible.

Once again we take our cue from St Paul. 'Forgetting what is behind and straining towards what is ahead, I press on towards the goal to win the prize for which God has called me heavenwards in Christ Jesus. All of us who are mature should take such a view of things' (Phil. 3:13–15).

# 10

# STICKING POINTS

Should anyone have assumed incorrectly that our ministry is always successful, we hasten to mention some common obstructions in the healing process. When any one of these becomes evident, the counsellor will require sensitivity to hear from God in order to identify the reason for the blockage. Then he will need to help the counsellee to deal with it. Some of the commonest sticking-points that we have encountered are listed below.

## 1 The inability to get in touch with feelings

People will often tell a horror story of some childhood abuse in a flat voice and with a completely dead-pan expression on the face. They appear to have switched off and at some time they have decided not to feel. Time and patience are needed with them. The following approach may be of help.

(a) It is vital to build a bridge of confidence. Long ago such people gave up trusting anyone. In order to immunise themselves from further pain they will commit themselves to no man. Before any healing can begin this bridge must be built.

(b) It is important to encourage them to face up to the reality of their hurts by talking about them. Try getting them to describe their experiences and then ask how they feel about them. Sometimes talking about a recent hurtful experience can trigger off suppressed feelings out of the past and in this way the counsellee is helped to make a connection with the suppressed childhood pain.

(c) Any inner vows they have made, such as: 'I will never permit myself to cry', 'I will never allow myself to feel' – should be renounced and formally broken.

(d) The Holy Spirit can be asked to bring any pain to the surface so that He can begin to heal it.

(e) A well-defended counsellee may be helped to become more open by adopting a physical stance of openness i.e. lying back in a chair with hands open and resting on the lap.

## 2 The inability to receive healing

Some people are able to express emotion but don't seem able to get beyond the bad feelings.

The hold-up could be caused by:

(a) **Fear.** As pain begins to surface, fear of that feeling will rise simultaneously to prevent its being fully expressed. The experience is sometimes accompanied by such physical manifestations as shaking, swallowing, headaches, stomach-ache, tears, groaning or hyperventilating. Continual reassurance and support is needed at this time. The counsellee should be encouraged to give vent to the pain and not to suppress it. God will often provide the counsellor with some insight that will open the floodgates, maybe (but not necessarily) through a 'word of knowledge'. On one occasion in our church there was a young lady whose body became physically locked into one position; she found herself unable to express anything. The rising pain was from the childhood loss of her grandfather who had been a major focus at that time for her security needs. It seemed right to those praying for her to ask an older male counsellor to take the young lady on his lap and rock her. This proved to be the trigger needed to unlock and surface the feelings.

Acknowledging and expressing pain diminishes its power

to hurt us. Healing and freedom come when, supported by praying friends, and in the presence of a Saviour who carried our sorrows (Isa. 53:4) and even suffered dereliction (Matt. 27:46) on our behalf, we are enabled to face the unnamed terror and live.

**(b) Anger**. Any hurtful experience produces anger towards those responsible for causing it. This may be expressed with tremendous energy, and, because of the release such an outburst may bring, there is a temptation to assume that the hurt has been thoroughly dealt with. But, as with the treatment of a septic finger, it is not enough to cleanse the wound of pus which might bring temporary relief; the foreign object which causes the pus must be extracted or the finger will remain infected. In such a way anger surrounds deep hurt.

In his book *The Primal Revolution*, Arthur Janov classifies 'anger and fear as secondary feelings . . . Secondary feelings overlie basic feelings and serve to block them.' The basic feelings are for safety, protection, value, identity, etc.

Once a young girl was receiving prayer for a bad relationship with her mother. She was tormented by the memory of a time of great need when she was a small child and her mother failed to come to her aid. Feelings of anger suddenly overwhelmed her and she shouted repeatedly, 'I hate you for not coming!' For a while it seemed that the venting of those strong feelings was helping her and healing would follow, but in fact there was a further stage in the healing process. Under the anger lay the terror of having been left alone to cope in a situation beyond a child's understanding. As the girl was encouraged to stay with the memory and continue to express the feelings, she began to cry in anguish, 'Mummy, please come. I need you to be here.' The basic unmet need for security was now being exposed and expressed. As all the pain was emptied out she was able to release forgiveness from the heart and invite the healing presence of Jesus to come.

**(c) False hope.** Below the anger and pain of loss is 'an unsuspecting hopeful foetus still holding on to its original shopping list' (Frank Lake, *Tight Corners in Pastoral Counselling*). We were all born with a list of needs – to be loved, to be valued, to be held, to be heard, to be protected, to be significant, etc. If those needs were not met, or were insufficiently met, a small part in us goes on searching hopefully. Hope is hard to give up. 'Hope springs eternal in the human breast,' but the painful reality may be that those needs were never met by a mother or a father. Another painful reality is that no one, either in the present or the future, will ever be able to meet those deprived needs fully. At some point this reality must be both faced and accepted and the direction of our hope changed.

It is as if we are in a room with two doors at opposite ends. One door is marked 'Man' and the other 'God'. As long as we wait hopefully facing the one marked 'Man', continual disappointment and pain will result. Only as we deliberately turn and face the door marked 'God' will there be hope for healing in our lives.

The counsellor needs to be very sensitive in helping the counsellee decide to turn. The glorious truth is that as we turn to God to meet our deepest needs we find ourselves becoming more integrated members of the Body of Christ in the process. The love of our spiritual brothers and sisters in Christ flows out to us in healing, as it should also begin to flow out from us in healing others.

**(d) Avoidance of responsibility.** Should the counsellor find that every session terminates with his feeling guilty, it could be that the counsellee is subtly avoiding responsibility which he has succeeded in shifting on to the counsellor. The counsellee is consciously agreeing to the discipline, but unconsciously really holding others to be responsible. There are various ways of detecting this tendency. Behaviour changes suggested by the counsellor are usually greeted with a 'Yes, but . . .' On the one hand the counsellee is consenting to change, but on the other he finds good reasons for not doing so. When the counsellor tries to point out some irrational belief or wrong behaviour adopted to meet his needs, the counsellee will change the subject and raise a different problem.

The counsellee departs looking more miserable than when he came, transmitting the unspoken message, 'You've made me feel worse – you are pushing me too far – you are pressing me too hard.'

Another way of avoiding responsibility is self-pity. At any point a counsellee may resort to this. He may have his good reasons, but to indulge in it will delay the healing process. Bouts of self-pity siphon off the energy needed to find solutions for the problems he faces. It is quite normal for a counsellee to sink into self-pity occasionally. It is unhealthy, however, to follow that route for long. He should be encouraged to move on.

If the counsellee refuses to face up to this behaviour pattern there is very little point in continuing. Nevertheless, once it is acknowledged and there is real commitment to change, good progress can be made.

**(e) Becoming hooked into counselling.** Counselling is all about loving help for hurting people. It is understandable, then, that a hurting person can become temporarily stuck under a counselling umbrella, where he feels cared for and protected. He may easily find himself hooked into being ministered to and lose his original goal for becoming whole. To be healed would be to chance losing that loving care. It would mean having to take up the challenge of standing on his own feet and of participating fully in life. To keep the counsellors' attention this person may get partially well in order to encourage them to continue the ministry. For this reason it is always helpful to make some stipulations at the beginning of ministry. The counsellee needs to know that there is going to be a time for assessment. In most cases, providing there was an original strong commitment to growth, this can be reactivated and the counsellee be encouraged to walk the road to healing once again.

**(f) The frostbite syndrome.** 'Neurosis is frozen pain' (*Primal Scream*, Janov).

To avoid pain a person may have switched off emotionally. The inner vow has been 'I must not feel. To feel is to hurt.' As the love of Jesus is then applied to those frozen feelings, life returns and pain surfaces. The pain can be likened to that of a frostbitten limb coming to life. 'I'm feeling worse not better,' is the cry. For a while it may seem that the counsellee has become locked into pain and his healing has stagnated. Real life is full of pain. 'Neurosis is always a substitute for legitimate suffering' (Carl Jung). The original switch-off was to avoid legitimate suffering so a switch-on will automatically involve pain. The counsellee is in fact beginning to come alive – to become a fully feeling person.

**(g) Inability to change behaviour.** 'If a person doesn't change his behaviour his pain will return and he will grow disillusioned with therapy' (William Glasser, *Modern Therapies*). The difficulty stems from our emotions. Often the faulty thinking that has governed the behaviour has been corrected and healing received, but the feelings still react to the old beliefs not the new. The counsellee then finds it hard to change behaviour with the feelings pulling him backwards. The will of the counsellee must be put on the side of the healing and on the side of the truth. If this is done, gradually the feelings will follow. As someone has said, 'The will can go ahead by express, but the emotions sometimes travel by slow freight.'

For many years I maintained the irrational belief that my presence was an inconvenience to others. This had governed much of my behaviour, particularly my freedom to make spontaneous calls on my friends. During the course of counselling the root of the irrational belief was uncovered. The truth was spoken both to the child of the past and to the adult of the present. Now I am continually put in the position of making a choice. I can still respond to the irrational belief and make excuses for not visiting my friends, or I can respond to the new, updated information that I am of value and acceptable to God and to others. If I act on this new information, gradually my feelings will back the truth until old things will have passed away and behold, even this thing has become new!

**(h) Persistent playing 'the child'.** This is a game many people play because it serves their purpose well – that of gaining care and attention from others. They will continue playing the game as long as others reciprocate with the role of the caring 'parent'.

Jesus spoke the truth to those who came to Him and refused to play their games. For example the rich young ruler was left with a choice. He could leave his old ways behind him and follow Jesus or he could keep his wealth and forfeit the company of Jesus. In other words he could continue his life style (play his accustomed game), but in no way was Jesus going to help him or encourage him in it. Quite the opposite.

Neither should we encourage someone to play the 'child' game. The truth should be pointed out gently and firmly, leaving the person with the choice to move forward or stay put. He should be given the clear understanding that the counsellor has no intention of playing his game with him.

In his book, *Why Am I Afraid to tell You Who I Am?*, John Powell suggests that we all have patterned reactions to life situations (games). 'It helps very much to be aware of our patterned reactions – the games we play. If we become aware of these games, we may give them up.' He goes on to say

> The one thing that all of these games have in common is this: they defeat self-knowledge and destroy all possibility of honest self-communication with others. The price of victory is costly; there is little chance for such a person to

experience true interpersonal encounters, which alone can put him on the path to human growth and the fulness of human life.

It is true to say we do no one a favour by playing these games with them. Neither can we help anyone by brutally tearing down his defences against the truth that he is so afraid to face. We must show people a better way, pointing them lovingly in the right direction and even leading the way ourselves by being real, truthful and open people.

To get hung up on any of these sticking-points usually indicates the failure on the part of the counsellee to use one or more of the disciplines mentioned in Chapter 5. The counsellor continually needs to restate the disciplines and encourage their application.

With patience, sticking-points can usually be surmounted, but some have proved beyond our help. We shall turn now to the difficulties and dangers surrounding this ministry.

# 11

# DANGERS AND DIFFICULTIES

The inner-healing ministry is not, as some may have imagined, the panacea for all ills. Many have begun ministering with great enthusiasm and then given up in despair because they have started with the most depressed person in the church and failed! Some people, as we shall see, are definitely unsuitable candidates for this particular ministry. That is not to say they do not need help, but for them it may come simply in the form of loving relationships, straightforward biblical counselling sessions, or maybe referral to a professional.

In the inner-healing ministry mistakes will happen and not all pitfalls can be avoided. True Christian love, however, does 'cover over a multitude of sins' (1 Pet. 4:8) and though occasionally inadequate ministry has been given we have not heard of anyone actually damaged by the ministry they have received. It is sometimes helpful, however, to be forewarned of the sort of pitfalls to look for and if possible avoid.

## 1 Severe depression

A major danger in this ministry is trying to bite off more than one can chew! Once it is noised abroad that there is a healing ministry operating in your church many hurting people will come pleading for help. The need, however, does not always constitute the call of God for ministry. In Mark's Gospel we see that Jesus left Capernaum while everyone was still looking for him to help (Mark 1:37–8). With every request for our assistance we should ask ourselves such questions as: 'Is this the right moment?' or 'Am I the right person to minister in this situation?' or 'Is inner healing the most suitable ministry for this person?'

We are told to pray for all the saints (Eph. 6:18), but we are not told to counsel everyone. All are blessed by prayer, but not all are helped by inner-healing prayer. Some counsellors have found themselves overwhelmed and exhausted by people they should probably never have been ministering to in the first place. It is wise always to delay before agreeing to minister to a very needy person. Take a little time praying for guidance and consult with others before giving a reply either way.

It would be inadvisable to minister inner healing to someone suffering from:

(a) **Psychotic depression**. This is a condition where a person has split from reality and is living in a fantasy world, or having hallucinations, and is seeing things that are not there.

(b) **Manic depression.** This is a state in which a person experiences very big mood swings. One moment he is euphoric and the next in the blackest depression.

(c) **Severe depression with suicidal tendencies.** Many people going through a difficult time will say, 'I wish I was dead!' but may not be seriously contemplating suicide. The true 'suicidal' talks continually of taking his own life and probably has already attempted to do so on more than one occasion.

After private prayer and consultation with wise friends one may feel the call of God to care for a person falling into one of the three categories above. If this is so, the following suggestions may be helpful.

(a) Liaise with the doctor or psychiatrist and inform him that you are trying to support his patient. Take any advice he may give you.

**(b)** Pray daily for the counsellee privately in your own devotions.

**(c)** If he is willing, pray with him but keep the prayers gentle and direct. In the name of Jesus call the body, mind and emotions back into balance, and then bless the person with the peace of God.

If the person is suffering from a neurotic depression which means he is aware of reality but his ordinary functioning is impaired, do as the above, but in addition the counsellor could also try to help him:

**(a)** To identify his irrational beliefs.

**(b)** Search for the origins of these beliefs.

**(c)** Focus on the truth of God's Word and correct these irrational beliefs in the light of what the Bible teaches.

By supporting a person in prayer and giving him a solid biblical foundation for his life he may well improve sufficiently for one to begin ministering in the area of inner healing.

Time, patience, and gentleness will be required to help any severely depressed person to enter into fullness of life once again.

Ros, a young married woman in our church who has received counselling for some time, due to a quite severe depression, has been an encouragement to us. Recently she sent me the following poem and covering letter which tell their own story.

The enclosed poem was written when I was still very depressed. I will describe the circumstances around it because they were quite unusual.

I was feeling very desperate that night. I awoke in the early hours feeling suddenly more light – peaceful. Then a kind of film sequence unfolded. It wasn't a dream and it was extremely vivid. I was living through the film. At that time only the forest part of the 'journey' was my actual experience; the forest is obviously symbolic of my depression, past hurts, wrong choices, etc. It was as though the rest of the poem was then given to me as a promise of hope for the future.

It was all so vivid that I went downstairs and wrote the poem in the middle of the night!

I stayed in the 'forest' or on the edge of it for a long time afterwards. It wasn't until last autumn [1985] that the whole poem took on new meaning.

During a time of prayer ministry with Prue (my counsellor), I found myself back at the edge of the forest – living out that part of the poem – stepping on out into the field. It was a very remarkable morning.

All the long night
I wandered through the dark forest
Choosing paths
Which led me nowhere.
Scratched and bruised, I stumbled on
Until I fell defeated
In the accumulated years
Of decaying leaves,
Leaves of my past.

Then I saw a dim light,
Heard the faint sound
Of a voice saying
'Come'.

I found myself
On the edge of the forest
Blinded by the light
Of a sharp, wintry sun.

A vast field lay before me
A solitary tree in its midst
Surrounded by hills in the distance.

A pathway led meandering out of sight
From where I stood –
And still the voice said –
'Come'.

Tripping
Slipping
I dragged my bruised limbs
Along the path
Till I looked up and saw
Not a tree
But a Cross.

'Come to me,' He said;
'Give me your burdens,
Give me your life.'

'What can you want with me, Lord?'
I protested.

'I love you.
I want you as you are.'

So I lay down at the foot
Of that Cross
And looked up.

The Cross was gone
And a man stood there,
Or rather a blinding radiance
Of gold
Which filled
Field, sky and the hills beyond.
A warmth surrounded me,
But I shivered –
Snow was falling now –

The earth which one moment
Was bathed
In golden light
Was now clothed
In dazzling white –
Pure,
Cleansing whiteness.

He wrapped something around me,
A white fur-skin
Roughly made
But thick, soft
And so warm.
He held me close
And together we set off
Making no footsteps
In the pristine snow.
'You are safe now,' He said.
'You will be battered by hail and snow
And wind and rain;
You will not see a path always
And night will come.
There are mountains to climb
And beasts that prey on you.
If you will stay close to me
You will become part of me.
Your footsteps will become my footsteps,
Your thoughts, my thoughts;
And I will be your shield
Against the sleet and the wind.
Mine will be the arm
That raises you from the mud.
I will be your guide
Through the mountain passes,
I will be your protection
From the wild beasts that prowl;

I will be your shelter and your sustenance.
You need only me
Because only in me
Is HOPE and LIFE.'

## 2 Demon Possession

People can be afflicted or troubled in some way by evil spirits
and providing one is working with a partner this can be dealt
with straightforwardly in the course of ministry and should
not be a difficulty. However, if a person is obviously
controlled by a demon that manifests itself violently, the case
should be referred to the minister or priest in charge of the
church.

## 3 Obsessions, Compulsions and Phobias

Other people we have found difficult to minister to are those
suffering from obsessive or compulsive behaviour problems
and those with phobias. A person in the grip of compulsive
behaviour seems to be in a vicious circle. Anxiety triggers off
the compulsion, and yielding to the compulsion then
produces more anxiety, and so on. We continue to wait on
God for answers to these problems, knowing that 'with God
all things are possible.'

We have experienced some success in the case of phobias
where inner healing has helped. Behaviour therapy, which
aims at modifying present behaviour, is often useful in
treating such problems, but since this deals only with the
symptoms and not the causes behind them, the problem may
disappear for several months only to reappear when the
sufferer comes under any fresh kind of stress. Many people
have experienced a measure of help through the experience
of 'resting in the Spirit'. This phenomenon of being

overwhelmed when the power of the Holy Spirit comes upon a person can be very healing. Experiences resulting from this vary from person to person.

(a) Some people go down under the Spirit's power and remain on the floor for just a short time. Apart from the good sensations of having been touched by God and a feeling of peace, nothing more seems to have happened.

(b) Others go down and lie quietly, as if asleep, for varying periods of time. When we question them later, they speak of waves of warmth and love washing over them, which they have subsequently found to have strengthened them in some way. They seem to have more confidence and more trust in God's love and power. There may well have been some inner healing going on at an unconscious level during this time. Others have been conscious of traumatic memories surfacing and being healed. Yet others testify to a new freedom (a bondage has been broken or an inhibiting fear expulsed).

(c) Some go down and experience other physical manifestations on their bodies. This may extend from slight shaking to marked bouncing. It is possible that a person may have very little idea what is happening to him at this time. No definite emotions may be surfacing. But it has frequently been our experience that they do begin to do so over the next few days. It is as though God has pierced through a layer of defences into a deeper area of their being and something has been shaken loose. When this happens further ministry may be needed.

(d) Lastly, when yet others go down they may experience some emotional discomfort, causing a response in the body, i.e. stiffness, pain, sensations of tightness around the head, a feeling of weight on the chest, some difficulty in breathing, nausea, etc. In such cases prayer for inner healing would be appropriate.

On one occasion a rather overweight young woman went down on the floor during a meeting and rested there for three hours. During that time she intermittently cried and shook. We heard many months later that without anyone ministering specifically to any particular problem she had experienced some deliverance and healing of the memories. Also since then she has lost several stones in weight.

On another occasion a young man in our fellowship fell to the floor when having prayer for epilepsy. He lay looking as if he were dead. As I looked at him I remembered with relief that when Jesus delivered the epileptic, 'The boy looked so much like a corpse that many said, "He's dead."' (Mark 9:26). Our young man has not had any recurrence of the problem since that evening three-and-a-half years ago and his doctor has vouched for his improved health so that he is now allowed to ride a motor-bike. Yet another lady, a few weeks after such an experience, testified to an unhealthy bondage to her parents being broken and an abnormal fear of death having dispersed.

## 4 Hysterical reactions

Another problem we have encountered is the hysterical reaction of hyperventilation or blacking out. The surfacing of long-buried terrifying memories can cause a reaction of panic. People have cried out sometimes, 'I feel I am disintegrating' or 'I'm going to fall into a thousand pieces.' As soon as the counsellor realises that this is a possible reaction, he should start by encouraging the counsellee to meet with Jesus and once he is aware of His presence suggest that he take His hand. The counsellor can then coax him to go back with Jesus and face the fear little by little. It is best to take this very gently and slowly. If the fear begins to overcome the counsellee so that he begins to hyperventilate, stop the ministry until he calms down. Only continue when both counsellor and counsellee feel the time is right.

We are often asked if it is necessary for everyone to revisit the original hurt and express the feelings surrounding it in order for healing to be experienced. The answer is 'Not necessarily.' We believe God is able to move sovereignly upon us and heal us instantaneously of all our hang-ups and inner pains if He so wishes. However, to date, our experience has been that the Holy Spirit frequently uncovers the past root cause of a person's problem and then brings healing at that point. In the process, new understanding is gained and people are then enabled to make better choices in the present.

When the basic needs of a child are not met he fears he will die because of the pain, so he splits from his feelings. From this point he continues to live but not fully. Part of his 'feeling self' is buried. The consequent hurts of childhood, teens and adult life only serve to reinforce that original early trauma. For healing to occur, the person needs to revisit the place and time of the 'split' both mentally and emotionally and reconnect with those fearful buried feelings. An authentic experience of unearthly and facing buried pain will extract an emotional response. The THEN becomes NOW. It is as if that past experience is happening today, but this time without the shutdown. At last the buried feelings are being fully felt and expressed. Feeling the split-off emotional pain integrates the person and diminishes the pain. 'I have seen the worst that can happen to me and I am still here. The rest, whatever it is, I can endure' (Morris West, *Shoes of the Fisherman*). It is into this reality that Jesus brings His healing.

This is not the only path to inner healing. God does not lead everyone in the same direction. Some people experience a symbolic type of journey where they receive insights into their own inner person. This enables them to make new sound choices based on those insights.

In a loving and secure environment a child's basic needs are sufficiently met and the hurtful experiences of life can be fully felt as they are encountered. In such cases there will be no split-off, no buried pain. They are in touch with their feelings and can express them easily and appropriately, there may be a need to go over some specific memories, release forgiveness and receive healing. Generally, though, for these fortunate cases the road to maturity will be fairly straightforward without major obstacles.

## 5 Unhealthy introversion

In a church where ministry to one another is encouraged and where people are becoming more open to God and to one another there is always the danger of an unhealthy introversion. This may be countered in several ways.

(a) It should be recognised that there are some people, besides those already mentioned, who do not benefit from inner-healing prayer. Once this becomes apparent such a person should be discouraged from receiving this type of ministry. These people may be in touch with their emotions but not in a healthy way. They are able to express every feeling they have ever felt and a few more besides! The problem here is one of control. Objective counselling on the disciplines required to achieve this would be more helpful, in such cases, than prayer for inner healing especially the delay of gratification and balancing. Others who do not appear to benefit from this type of ministry are the already self-absorbed people. They are so taken up with themselves and their own inner workings that the ministry of inner healing only seems to increase their unhealthy introversion. Such people need help in extending themselves outwards towards the needs of others. They need to learn to give rather than to receive; to leave behind and press on rather than to look back and wallow in the mire of self-pity.

(b) There should be no pressure on anyone to seek inner healing. At the same time it should be available for those who are feeling God nudging them to get certain aspects of their lives sorted out, and would appear to be suitable candidates for this type of ministry. The responsibility for seeking help must rest with the individual. This seems to provide a much healthier approach and makes a successful outcome more likely.

(c) Encourage those receiving ministry not to delve around between sessions and not to allow their friends to do it for them. If feelings, memories or thoughts start surfacing involuntarily, or if they have vivid dreams, suggest that the counsellee keeps a notebook and writes down the information. This should then be left there until the next counselling session.

(d) Jesus said about healing, 'Freely you have received, freely give' (Matt. 10:8). When healing is evidently happening, encourage the counsellee to begin praying and ministering to others. They may begin by becoming involved in the Sunday ministry offered after both morning and evening services. Opportunities will soon follow out of this to minister more widely. We shall never be totally free of the dangers of imbalance, but the counterbalance to an unhealthy 'looking in' is a healthy 'looking out'.

## 6 Bizarre practices

Alongside unhealthy introversion is the danger of bizarre practices which may be simply an ego trip. We need constantly to re-examine what we are doing in the light of Scripture and effectiveness. Results are often difficult to assess in this ministry. Changes at such a deep level; may be slow to affect our day-to-day experience. Nevertheless, we must not draw back from asking ourselves if this kind of ministry is producing good fruit. Recently I was told by a friend of some ministry she had received from two people who did not stay around with her long enough to face up to its ineffectiveness. They thought they were ministering to the inner child of her past. When she was unable to make the connection with her past feelings, they had taken over and had wept and cried out for her. They had ventilated anger and resentment and had reckoned they were feeling my friend's inner pain for her. She felt nothing and was left having made no connection with her own suppressed pain and with no more idea of how she had reacted to those past feelings or the sort of action she had taken to protect herself against them. Perhaps the two counsellors had benefited from the cathartic experience of the ventilating on her behalf, but it was of no benefit to the counsellee whatsoever.

Just occasionally I have seen an enacted word of knowledge release some healing within a counsellee. For example, I was once present when someone enacted being locked in a cupboard, giving vent to the panic associated with that experience. This had in fact been the counsellee's experience and was a help in subsequent ministry to her. At the same time it bordered on the bizarre and I should have found it more helpful if it had been offered vocally and the counsellee then encouraged to experience her own feelings about that past event in her life.

The more the counsellee works at making his own connections with the past, taking responsibility for his own inner child, his own reactions and his resulting behaviour, the more growth will be experienced. It is all too easy to fall into the trap of keeping a person in some sort of dependent place and fail to encourage self-responsibility. The counsellor will need considerable self-discipline himself for this ministry. A continual openness to the examination of his own life and ministry is essential.

## 7 Misuse of confession

The misuse of confession can be another problem in a fellowship where people are anxious to be right with God and with their neighbour. The practice is biblical and, providing we are careful and take note of the warnings, can be of great blessing to the Body of Christ. James tells us to confess our sins to each other and pray for each other 'so that you may be healed' (Ja. 5:16).

The aim of confession is that we should know the forgiveness of God and be restored to wholeness in relationship to Him. It is also to restore a right relationship with others. To walk in the light with one another ensures that no root of bitterness is allowed to grow up in our fellowship with each other.

If relationship with God is impaired because of unconfessed sin, find a mature Christian and make a clear confession in his presence bearing in mind the following warnings.

(a) Make sure that the other person will not be harmed by your confession. Some sins should only be confessed to a married person of some maturity.

(b) Confession of sin should only be as public as the sin itself. If the sin has been committed in the presence of, or with the full knowledge of, a group of people, it would be best to confess it publicly. If it was a hidden sin, then confession is best made to one individual person.

(c) Beware of trying to impress others with the confession of gross sin. If relationship with another is impaired because of sin against him, confess your sin to him alone, asking for forgiveness, but bear in mind the following warnings.

(d) Beware of burdening another person in order simply to relieve oneself. A husband may have committed adultery and in confessing it to his partner cause her to suffer a loss of value and feelings of rejection. It may well be right for him to confess such a sin to his wife, but first he must be sure God is prompting him and that it is not just a desire to dump his burden on another unnecessarily. It may be better to confess the sin to a counsellor and not to the partner concerned.

(e) Take care not to leave someone under condemnation by subtly placing blame on him. Someone may have caused you hurt quite unintentionally and the feelings you have may be due to your own damaged emotions. By confessing your hurt and anger to that person you may place an unnecessary burden of guilt on him. In such a case deal with the fault either alone with God by releasing forgiveness to the person involved or go to a mature counsellor and deal with it before God together.

## Conclusion

Despite these dangers and difficulties, we have been encouraged to continue developing this ministry. So many people – young, old, male and female – are imprisoned by their past. They need some help to leave their past behind and enter into the inheritance that God has for them as sons and daughters of the King.

It would be easy to tell them to 'pull yourself together' or to 'just have faith and believe God's promises'. For too many years this has been the only counsel they have received from the Christian family. In desperation some have sought secular counselling, but many others have just continued to suppress their problems and avoid those situations which might make them vulnerable. 'No one in my church knows; I could never share it with them' is the sad comment we hear all too frequently. We are well aware of our own inadequacy in many areas and still have so much to learn, but we are always endeavouring to become better equipped. Our greatest limitation seems to be that of time and energy. Our prayer is that many more churches will begin to 'equip their saints for works of service', in particular the ministry of inner healing.

# SOME RECOMMENDED READING

This is not intended to be an exhaustive list, but an indication of some of the books I have found helpful.

Rita Bennett, *Emotionally Free* (Kingsway)

Rita Bennett, *How to Pray for Inner Healing* (Kingsway)

John Cleese and Robin Skynner, *Families and How to Survive Them* (Methuen)

Lawrence J. Crabb, *Basic Principles of Biblical Counselling* (Marshalls)

Theodore Elliott Dobson, *Inner Healing, God's Great Assurance* (Paulist Press)

Reginald East, *Heal the Sick* (Hodder & Stoughton)

Ruth Fowke, *Beginning Pastoral Counselling* (Grove Books)

Jim Glennon, *Your Healing is Within You* (Hodder & Stoughton)

Jean Grigo, *Grow to Love* (St Andrew's Press)

Selwyn Hughes, *A Friend In Need* (Kingsway)

Roger Hurding, *Roots and Shoots* (Hodder & Stoughton)

Arthur Janov, *The Primal Revolution* (Sphere)

Frank Lake, *Tight Corners in Pastoral Counselling* (Dalton, Longman & Todd)

Frank Lake, *Clinical Theology,* abridged by Martin H. Yeomans (Darton, Longman & Todd)

Dennis and Matthew Linn, *Healing Life's Hurts* (Paulist Press)

Francis MacNutt, *Healing* (Ave Maria Press)

Dr M. Scott Peck, *The Road Less Travelled* (Hutchinson)

Dr M. Scott Peck, *A People of the Lie* (Hutchinson)

John Powell, *Why Am I Afraid to Love?* (Fontana)

John Powell, *Why Am I Afraid to Tell You Who I Am?* (Fontana)

David Pytches, *Come, Holy Spirit* (Hodder & Stoughton)

John and Paula Sandford, *Transformation of the Inner Man* (Logos)

David Seamands, *Healing for Damaged Emotions* (Victor Books)

David Seamands, *Healing of the Memories* (Victor Books)

David Seamands, *Putting Away Childish Things* (Victor Books)

*Further books from Hodder & Stoughton on ministering healing and wholeness*

# A HEALING FELLOWSHIP

## By Mary Pytches

What makes for 'safe' counselling? What boundaries and limits must be built around the counselling relationship? How do you distinguish between demonisation and psychological trauma? Is inner healing biblical?

Drawing on her years of counselling experience at St Andrew's, Chorleywood, where her husband, David, is Vicar, Mary Pytches provides practical guidelines for any church or individual wishing to enter into this ministry. The importance of the church community is emphasised whilst she looks in detail at the nature of the relationship between counseller and counsellee. Mary Pytches describes the need for a 'safe place' to be found in which counselling can take place. St Andrew's is seeking to be a true community where – in today's hurting world – fellowship and healing may be found.

'Over the years I have come to realise that of all the areas of healing that I have been involved in, inner healing is the most needed by suffering humanity. Mary Pytches combines her wealth of experience as a counsellor with her prayer ministry in a very clear and practical way. I find her book most helpful and I highly recommend it.'

*Francis MacNutt*

# COME, HOLY SPIRIT

## David Pytches

Many churches today are seeking and experiencing spiritual renewal. *Come, Holy Spirit* is a comprehensive and practical guide to ministering in the power of the Holy Spirit.

Outlining and exploring each of the gifts of the Holy Spirit, David Pytches provides a firm biblical basis for their practice, along with illuminating illustrations of their use. Chapters are devoted to other areas of ministry which include ministering to dying people and their families, ministering to children, the centrality of worship and the place of liturgy. Examining the way in which Jesus ministered on earth, David Pytches discusses questions of wholeness, authority and power, as well as the reasons why people are not healed.

'Already a very popular bestseller, (it) will become the handbook for many.'        *Church of England Newspaper*

'Get this book: it is a goldmine.'        *Anglicans for Renewal*

'Will encourage and challenge.'        *Buzz*

David Pytches, formerly Bishop of Chile, Bolivia and Peru, is currently Vicar of St Andrew's, Chorleywood in Hertfordshire.

# POWER HEALING

## John Wimber

Healing is high on the agenda in many churches in the eighties. John Wimber tackles this controversial topic by constructing a practical theology of healing.

In particular he
- presents compelling biblical arguments for the practice of a healing ministry, particularly relating to physical healing
- answers difficult questions such as 'Why isn't everybody healed?'
- provides suggestions for equipping Christians to pray effectively for healing.

*Power Healing* is structured around John Wimber's personal testimony from his calling to a healing ministry, the barren years during which no-one was healed, to his current international ministry.

*John Wimber* is the charismatic founding pastor of the Vineyard Christian Fellowship. His first book *Power Evangelism* has been widely acclaimed.

# DOES JESUS CARE?

## R T Kendall

'Do you know the feeling of being completely let down by the one you thought was the only person that could help you? What if that last resort was Jesus?'

Perhaps a loved one dies despite earnest prayer, a job falls through, or plans collapse even after prayerful preparation. Jesus seems far away. Does he really care?

'Yes,' affirms R T Kendall. 'This book will show not only that he cares but that he cares more deeply and painstakingly than you or I can begin to imagine. Nothing is too hard for the Lord and nothing shall be impossible with God.'

DOES JESUS CARE? speaks to the heart of disappointment, bringing understanding and renewing faith.

Dr R T Kendall is minister of Westminster Chapel, and author of *Tithing* and *Once Saved, Always Saved*.